HOUGHTON MIFFLIN

California Science

Study Guide
Student Workbook

Main Idea Worksheets

Lesson Science Vocabulary Worksheets

Lesson Support Vocabulary Worksheets

 HOUGHTON MIFFLIN   BOSTON

Printed in the United States of America

ISBN 13: 978-0-618-93775-2
ISBN 10: 0-618-93775-7

22 0928 19
4500752544

 HOUGHTON MIFFLIN   BOSTON

Contents

Unit D Electricity and Magnetism

Study Guide
Student Workbook

What Are Nonliving Parts of Ecosystems?

Main Idea Nonliving parts of an ecosystem, such as water, air, and sunlight, help living things meet their basic needs.

- Ecosystems are made up of living and nonliving things.

- Each ecosystem has its own set of nonliving parts, which include light, water, temperature, and soil.

- The conditions of water, air, temperature, and light in an ecosystem determine which living things can live there.

A. Complete the chart to tell how nonliving things help living things meet their basic needs.

Nonliving Thing	How It Helps Living Things
soil	_____
light	_____
	_____
air	_____
water	_____

B. Replace the underlined words and phrases with the correct words and phrases to tell how differences in nonliving things affect ecosystems.

The conditions of nonliving things in different ecosystems are
<u>the same</u> _____. For example, the form of <u>sunlight</u>
_____ in an ecosystem may be different. The <u>body</u>
_____ temperature may be higher in some ecosystems
and lower in others.

Use with pages 6–11

What Are Nonliving Parts of Ecosystems?

C. Label each drawing below to tell the type of ecosystem shown.

ice sheet

1. _____

shade trees

2. _____

high daytime temperatures

3. _____

4. How are these ecosystems similar?
How are they different?

_____

_____

_____

_____

_____

_____

What Are Nonliving Parts of Ecosystems?

ecosystem

Complete the diagram by providing details about what an
ecosystem is.

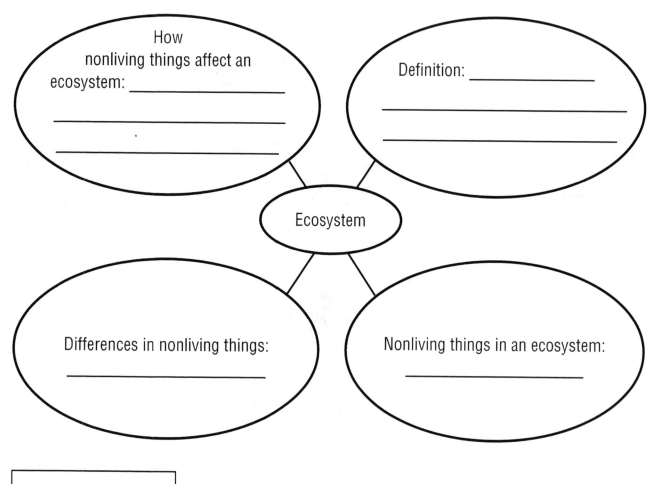

How
nonliving things affect an
ecosystem: _____
_____
_____

Definition: _____
_____
_____

Ecosystem

Differences in nonliving things:
_____

Nonliving things in an ecosystem:
_____

**Vocabulary Skill:
Prefix/Suffix**

The prefix *eco-* means "environment." How does knowing the meaning
of the prefix *eco-* help you understand the meaning of the word *ecosystem?*

_____

_____

_____

What Are Nonliving Parts of Ecosystems?

Glossary

life processes	activities that all living things do in their ecosystems
shade	protection from direct sunlight provided by some plants, such as trees
soil	the loose top layer of Earth's surface
temperature	how hot or cold something is

Complete the diagram using words from the box.

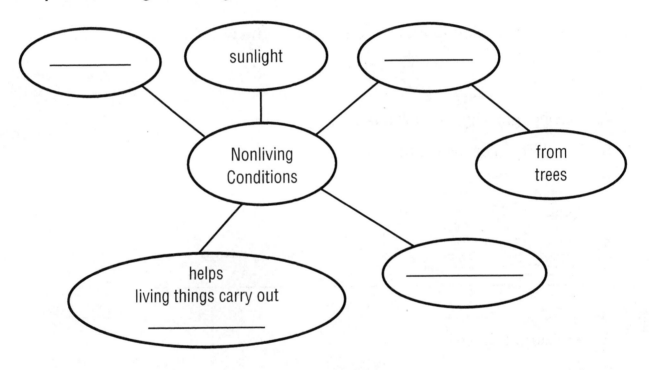

Homework: Write two or three sentences explaining how nonliving parts of an ecosystem help living things meet their needs. Include at least three words from the box.

What Are Living Parts of Ecosystems?

Main Idea Living things depend on nonliving things to meet their basic needs. Different plants and animals meet their needs in different ecosystems.

- The nonliving and living things in an ecosystem help organisms carry out life processes.

- A community, which is all the living things in one area, is supported by the nonliving conditions of its ecosystem.

- Organisms live in the conditions that best meet their needs.

A. Complete the outline to identify and explain the basic needs of living things.

I. _____

    A. moving, growing, breathing require it

    B. the ability to cause change

    C. _____

II. Nutrients

    A. _____

    _____

III. _____

    A. a mixture of gases

    B. oxygen

IV. _____

    A. a place to live

    B. provides protection from other animals

V. Water

    A. _____

    B. _____

What Are Living Parts of Ecosystems?

**B. Complete the diagram to describe life processes that
organisms carry out in ecosystems.**

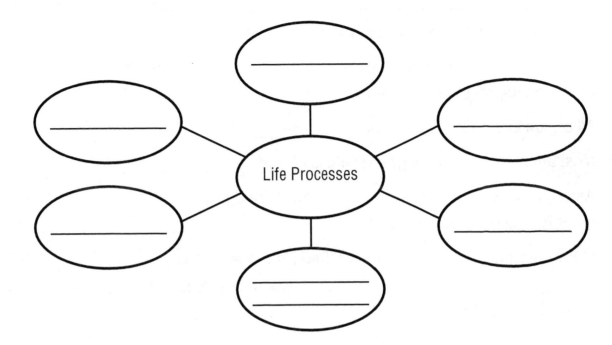

**C. Place a check mark next to each statement that is
true about organisms in ecosystems.**

_____ 1. All the members of one kind of plant or animal in a
community make up a population.

_____ 2. An organism will survive only in an environment that meets
it needs.

_____ 3. All the organisms in an ecosystem make up a community.

_____ 4. Different parts of an ecosystem have the same conditions.

_____ 5. Organisms can meet their needs in all areas of the
ecosystem in which they live.

Study Guide

7

Use with pages 12–19

What Are Living Parts of Ecosystems?

community	energy	environment	organism
oxygen	population	reproduce	temperate zone

A. Use a word from the box to complete each sentence.

1. All living things have the ability to _____; that is, produce offspring like themselves.

2. All organisms need a source of _____.

3. Most animals also need a gas in air called _____.

4. An organism's _____ must meet its needs in order for the organism to survive.

5. Many different organisms carry out their life processes in a _____, an area of Earth where the temperature rarely gets very hot or very cold.

B. Think about the relationship between the terms *community*, *organism*, and *population*. Use these words to complete the diagram to show the levels of living things in an ecosystem.

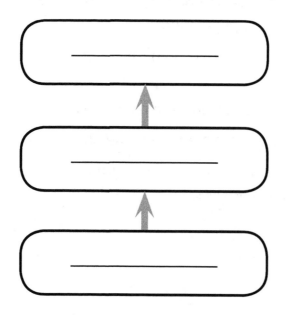

Study Guide
8
Use with pages 12–19

What Are Living Parts of Ecosystems?

Glossary

basic needs	what organisms must meet to stay alive
conditions	factors of the environment
shelter	place that keeps an organism safe
traits	characteristics of a living thing
waste	material leftover after a process

Cross out the incorrect word in each sentence and replace it with a correct word from the box.

1. Living things use nonliving things to meet their goals

   _____.

2. Some byproducts _____ of living things include breathing and moving.

3. Plants take in the gas carbon dioxide, whereas animals give off carbon dioxide as energy _____.

4. All animals need a home, or niche _____.

5. An organism lives in the part of an ecosystem where the nonliving organisms _____ best meet its needs.

Homework: Choose an animal that you know. Write about how the animal uses nonliving things to survive. Include at least three words from the box.

What Are Some Land Ecosystems?

Main Idea The nonliving conditions of each land ecosystem help determine which plants and animals can survive there.

- Different land ecosystems have different nonliving conditions.
- Every land ecosystem has its own set of animals and plants and nonliving conditions.
- The environment of different land ecosystems gives organisms the things they need to survive.

A. Complete the chart to describe the four land ecosystems.

Land Ecosystem	Description	Conditions	Location
rainforest	an ecosystem where it rains a lot		
desert			
chaparral			
taiga			

What Are Some Land Ecosystems?

B. Place a check mark next to all the statements that are true about some land ecosystems.

_____ **1.** The nonliving conditions are the same in each area of a tropical rainforest.

_____ **2.** All deserts support the same plant and animal communities.

_____ **3.** Taiga and rainforests support many trees.

_____ **4.** Because tropical rainforests are home to so many plants, they produce a lot of Earth's oxygen.

_____ **5.** Wildfires are common in chaparral communities.

C. Fill in the diagram to show where each of the following organisms lives.

coast horned lizard	scrub jay
desert tortoise	road runner
fire-resistant oaks, pines, and brush	spruce tree
howler monkey	toucan
jaguar	tree frog
Kopok tree	wolf
moose	

Four Land Ecosystems

Tropical Rainforest	Desert	Chaparral	Taiga
_____	_____	coast horned lizard	_____
_____	_____	_____	_____
_____		_____	
_____			

What Are Some Land Ecosystems?

chaparral   communities   desert
ecosystem   rainforest   taiga

Use words from the box to complete the sentences about ecosystems.

1. A land _____ may get a lot of rain or very
   little rain.

2. A(n) _____ is an area where it rains a lot.

3. A(n) _____ ecosystem gets little rain.

4. Because the nonliving conditions in rainforests and deserts
   are different, these ecosystems support different plant and
   animal _____.

5. Animals of another land ecosystem, called the
   _____, can survive wet, mild winters
   and extremely hot, dry summers.

6. The _____, a fairly dry ecosystem, receives
   most of its moisture in the form of snow.

Homework: Research California's chaparral ecosystem and write
a paragraph summarizing what you learned. Be sure to include
the conditions of the ecosystem and the kinds of organisms that
live there.

What Are Some Land Ecosystems?

Glossary

adapted	suited to survive and reproduce
fire-resistant	able to survive fire
nonliving conditions	set of nonliving parts of an ecosystem
nutrients	materials in food and soil that living things need for energy and growth
oxygen	gas in air that most living things need to survive

Complete the chart using words from the box to tell about different ecosystems. Hint: You will use one of the descriptions for all four ecosystems.

1. _____	Evergreens are _____ to cold, dry nonliving conditions.
2. _____	_____ oaks can survive wildfires, which are common.
3. _____ _____	_____ help determine which plants and animals survive.
4. _____	The soil has few _____.
5. _____	These ecosystems produce a lot of Earth's _____.

What Are Some Water Ecosystems?

Main Idea The different nonliving conditions of each water ecosystem help determine what organisms can survive there.

- Different water ecosystems have their own sets of animals, plants, and nonliving conditions.

- Saltwater ecosystems include shorelines, the coastal ocean, coral reefs, and the open ocean.

- Freshwater ecosystems include streams, rivers, ponds, lakes, and wetlands.

A. Complete the diagram to classify water ecosystems using the words from the box. Then answer the question that follows.

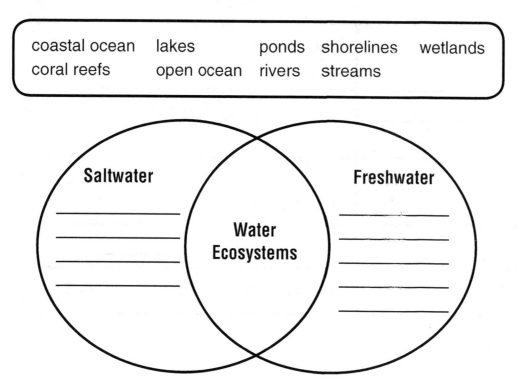

coastal ocean   lakes   ponds   shorelines   wetlands

coral reefs   open ocean   rivers   streams

Saltwater   Water Ecosystems   Freshwater

Why do different water ecosystems have their own sets of animals and plants?

_____

_____

What Are Some Water Ecosystems?

B. Complete each sentence to tell about saltwater and freshwater ecosystems.

1. In an ocean ecosystem, the shoreline is covered by

   _____ or exposed to _____ .

2. A coral reef is an ecosystem found in _____

   and built on a structure of _____ .

3. _____ does not reach very far down into the

   open ocean, so most of it is very _____ and very

   _____ .

4. Streams and rivers have water that _____ .

5. Ponds and lakes are made of _____ .

C. Complete the chart to compare nonliving conditions and organisms in the three areas of deep ponds and lakes in freshwater ecosystems.

Area	Water Temperatures	Organisms
_____	warmest water	_____
below the surface	cooler water	_____ _____
deep water	_____	organisms that break down dead plants and animals

What Are Some Water Ecosystems?

(coral reef)

Complete the diagram with details about coral reefs.

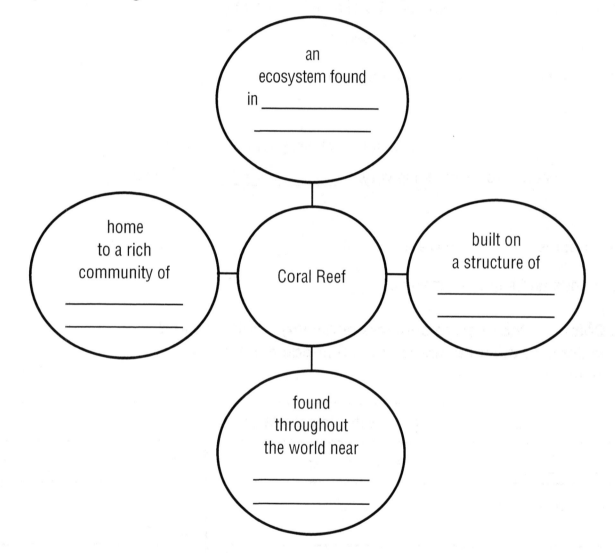

Homework: Imagine you are visiting a coral reef. Make a postcard for a friend. On the front, paint or draw a color picture of the reef. On the back, describe the living and nonliving parts of the ecosystem.

What Are Some Water Ecosystems?

Glossary

coastal ocean	part of the ocean just beyond the shoreline
freshwater	water that is not salty
open ocean	part of the ocean beyond the coastal ocean
saltwater	water that contains a dissolved salt
shoreline	the edge of a body of water
underwater	under the surface of water

A. Use each of the words _freshwater, saltwater, shoreline,_ and _underwater_ in a sentence that tells about a water ecosystem.

_____

_____

_____

_____

_____

_____

B. Use each of the terms _coastal ocean_ and _open ocean_ in a sentence that tells about a water ecosystem.

_____

_____

_____

How Do Organisms Depend on Each Other?

Main Idea Living things in an ecosystem depend on one another for basic needs such as food, shelter, and protection.

- Every living thing has a role to play within an ecosystem.

- Animals depend on plants for food and sometimes for shelter.

- Many plants depend on animals to help them reproduce and disperse seeds.

A. Place a check mark next to all the statements that are true about interactions between organisms in ecosystems.

_____ **1.** Living things in an ecosystem are independent and rarely interact with each other.

_____ **2.** Each organism has a job to do in its environment.

_____ **3.** Without plants, other organisms in an ecosystem could not survive.

_____ **4.** All organisms meet their needs for food with the help of other organisms.

B. Complete the diagram to describe the relationships between organisms in an ecosystem.

the Sun

producer: _____   consumer: _____

_____   _____

_____   _____

How Do Organisms Depend on Each Other?

C. Put the events in order to tell about pollinators.

_____ As they feed, they carry pollen from flower to flower.

_____ When pollen carried on the pollinator touches the right part of the flower, seeds begin to form.

_____ The plant produces pollen.

_____ Pollinators feed on the pollen and nectar of plants.

D. Complete the diagram to tell about seed dispersal.

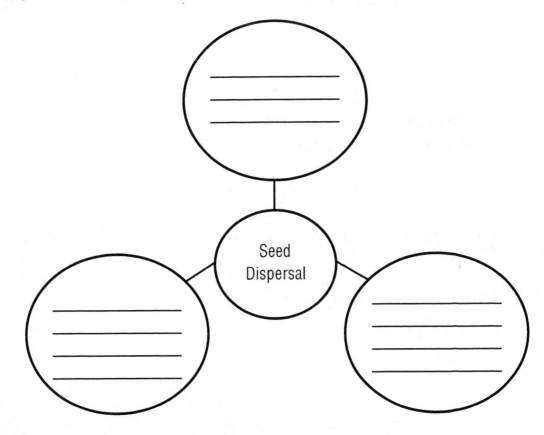

Homework: Make a diagram that shows how animals help plants reproduce.

How Do Organisms Depend on Each Other?

consumer   pollinator
producer   seed dispersal

Complete the diagram with words from the box.

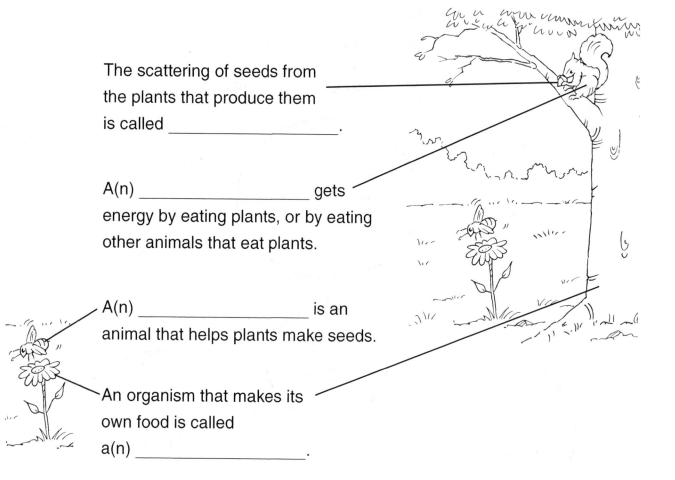

The scattering of seeds from the plants that produce them is called _____.

A(n) _____ gets energy by eating plants, or by eating other animals that eat plants.

A(n) _____ is an animal that helps plants make seeds.

An organism that makes its own food is called a(n) _____.

How Do Organisms Depend on Each Other?

Glossary

benefit	to be helped by
protection	state of being covered or shielded from harm
relationship	way in which organisms are connected to each other
roles	functions

Fill in the caption using words from the box.

The clown fish (a consumer) and sea anemone
(a producer) have different _____
in their ecosystem. Both organisms _____
from their _____ with each other.
The fish gets _____ against its enemies,
which avoid the anemone's poisonous tentacles.
The anemone gets a bath: The fish eats scraps of food
that cling to the tentacles.

**Vocabulary Strategy:
Sentence Context**

When you come upon an unknown word, you can sometimes
use the other words in the sentence to determine the meaning.
What is the meaning of the word *transferred* in this sentence?
Underline the other words in the sentence that helped you.

When an animal eats a plant, energy in the plant is transferred
to the animal.

_____

Use with pages 46–53

How Are Organisms Adapted to Survive?

Main Idea To survive, plants and animals must be adapted to their environment. Their adaptations help organisms obtain food, hide from other animals, and generally survive the conditions of their environment.

- Plants and animals have adaptations that help them meet their needs. Adaptations can be physical features or behaviors.

- A species may or may not be able to adapt to changes in its environment.

- A species that is not able to adapt to changes in its environment may become extinct.

A. Complete the diagram to classify and explain adaptations that help organisms survive in their environment.

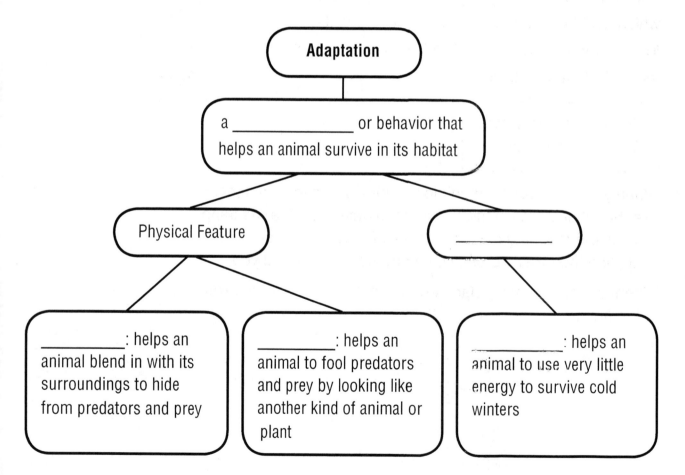

How Are Organisms Adapted to Survive?

B. Place a check mark next to each statement that is true about how organisms are affected by changes in their habitats.

_____ 1. Organisms rely on their habitat to provide everything they need to survive.

_____ 2. All organisms in a habitat can equally survive changes in their habitat.

_____ 3. Organisms adapted to live in very specific habitats have difficulty meeting their needs if that habitat changes.

_____ 4. Any species can become extinct when it is unable to adapt to changes in its habitat.

_____ 5. Habitat destruction is one of the biggest threats to species all over the world.

C. Complete the diagram to tell about the giant panda and its difficulty in adapting to its changing habitat.

The giant panda eats _____ _____.

Bamboo forests in China, where the panda lives, have _____.

The giant panda is in danger because _____ _____ _____.

How Are Organisms Adapted to Survive?

adaptation   camouflage   habitat
hibernate   mimicry   predator
prey   species

Match each word from the box with its definition.

_____ **1.** animal that is hunted for food by a predator

_____ **2.** physical feature or behavior that helps an
organism survive

_____ **3.** go into a deep sleep, during which very little
energy is used

_____ **4.** physical appearance of an animal that helps it
blend in with its surroundings

_____ **5.** animal that hunts other animals for food

_____ **6.** group of organisms that produces organisms of
the same kind

_____ **7.** adaptation that allows an animal to protect itself by
looking like another kind of animal or like a plant

_____ **8.** place where a plant or animal lives

Homework: Write one or two paragraphs explaining how animals are
adapted to survive in their environments. Use at least six words from
the box.

How Are Organisms Adapted to Survive?

Glossary

appearance	the way something looks or appears; outward aspect
behavior	the way in which something behaves; conduct
dramatically	arresting or forceful in appearance or effect
survive	to stay alive or in existence
surroundings	the things that affect and surround one

Use the words from the box to complete each sentence. Then circle each word in the puzzle.

```
Y  O  J  E  V  I  V  R  U  S  Q  S
R  K  U  C  S  Z  N  P  L  S  I  L
P  A  Z  N  Q  T  G  Z  K  Z  O  M
Y  L  L  A  C  I  T  A  M  A  R  D
S  U  R  R  O  U  N  D  I  N  G  S
G  K  S  A  P  V  U  G  Q  S  K  T
E  R  B  E  H  A  V  I  O  R  A  Q
A  Z  S  P  K  L  S  Z  R  T  N  L
Q  E  J  P  A  T  G  L  A  O  E  P
U  P  G  A  R  N  S  S  I  L  G  M
```

1. An adaptation helps an animal _____ in its habitat.

2. An animal's physical _____ can help it hide from predators.

3. _____, as well as appearance, can help a predator as it hunts for prey.

4. Mimicry allows an animal to protect itself by looking like another animal; camouflage helps an animal blend in with its

_____ .

5. If an organism's habitat changes _____ , the organism may or may not meet its basic needs.

How Do Organisms Compete?

Main Idea Food, air, water, and living space are limited in any ecosystem. To survive, organisms compete for these resources.

- A balanced ecosystem has enough resources for all its living things.
- The populations of predators and prey are balanced in a healthy ecosystem.

A. Place a check next to all the statements that are true about how living things compete.

_____ **1.** To survive, every organism needs water, air, food, and living space.

_____ **2.** Resources that organisms need to meet their basic needs are limited.

_____ **3.** Plants and animals compete for food and water, but not for space.

_____ **4.** If there is not enough prey in an ecosystem, animals that rely on that prey for food will survive on something else.

_____ **5.** Populations in any ecosystem are always changing.

_____ **6.** Populations change when old animals die and new ones take their place.

_____ **7.** Sometimes the balance in an ecosystem can be upset.

_____ **8.** In a healthy ecosystem, the populations of prey and the populations of predators are balanced.

Use with pages 66–71

How Do Organisms Compete?

B. Complete the diagram to show how limited resources affect the organisms in an ecosystem.

In a plant population...

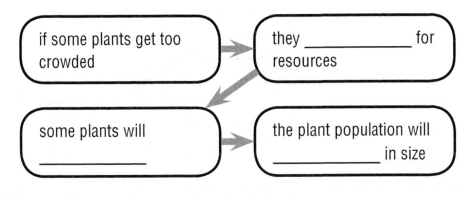

if some plants get too crowded

they _____ for resources

some plants will _____

the plant population will _____ in size

C. Complete the diagram to show how ecosystems remain in balance.

In an animal population...

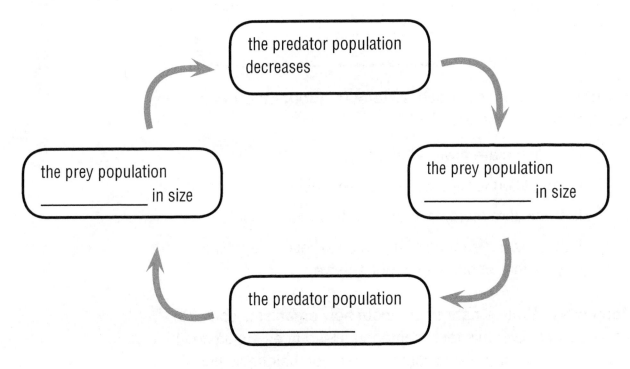

the predator population decreases

the prey population _____ in size

the prey population _____ in size

the predator population _____

How Do Organisms Compete?

resource

A. Complete the diagram to tell about resources.

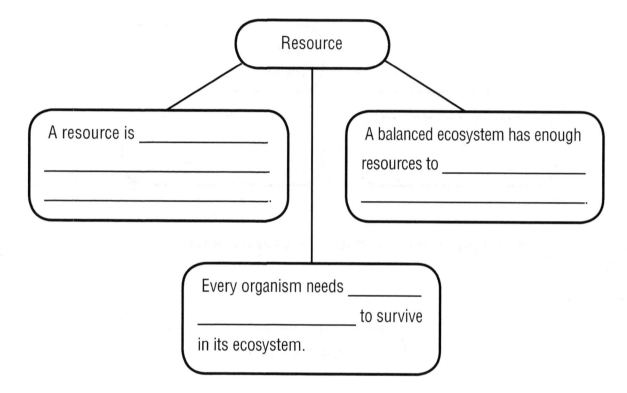

B. Put a check next to each statement about resources in an ecosystem that is true.

_____ Resources are always limited.

_____ Competition for space can cause a population to increase.

_____ In tropical rainforests, many plants must compete for sunlight.

_____ If there is not enough of a particular resource, animals that rely on the resource may not survive.

Homework: Write a paragraph about how organisms compete for resources. Use this topic sentence: Resources are limited in ecosystems, so organisms compete to meet their basic needs.

Study Guide
28
Use with pages 66–71

How Do Organisms Compete?

Glossary

balanced	even; in the right proportions
exposed	without protection; bare
limited	in short supply; not endless
protected	kept safe

The underlined word in each sentence is incorrect. Replace it with a word from the box.

1. A(n) <u>unbalanced</u> _____ ecosystem has enough resources to meet the needs of its living things.

2. Organisms compete for <u>unlimited</u> _____ resources in the ecosystem where they live.

3. For example, birds that lose the competition for space may be forced to raise their young in <u>unexposed</u> _____ nesting grounds.

4. Birds that succeed in the competition for space can raise their young among other birds in a(n) <u>unprotected</u> _____ colony.

> **Vocabulary Skill:**
> **Prefixes**

The prefix *ex-* mean "out" or "from." The root *-pos-* is from the Latin word *positus*, meaning "to put or set." Using your knowledge of the word parts, write your own definition of the word *exposed*.

_____

What Are Food Chains?

Main Idea In an ecosystem, energy flows from the Sun to producers and from producers to consumers.

- Plants use the Sun's energy to produce food. Some animals get energy by eating plants. Some animals get energy by eating other animals that eat plants.

- All plants and animals are part of a food chain.

- Less energy is available the further a population of organisms is from the producers in the chain.

A. Complete the diagram to tell about how plants and some animals get energy.

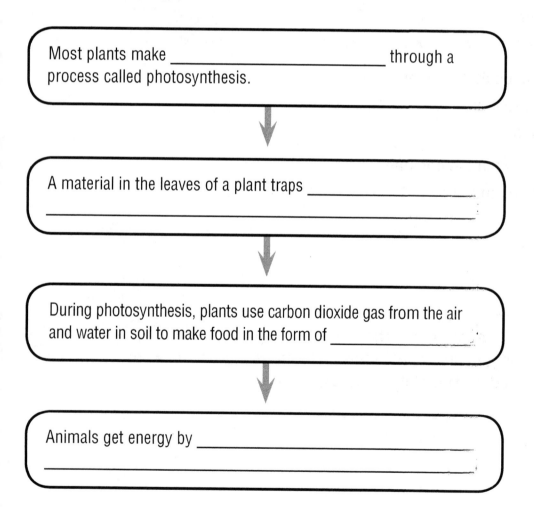

Most plants make _____ through a process called photosynthesis.

A material in the leaves of a plant traps _____
_____

During photosynthesis, plants use carbon dioxide gas from the air and water in soil to make food in the form of _____.

Animals get energy by _____
_____

What Are Food Chains?

B. Complete the chart to tell about links in a food chain.

Animal	Definition	Example
herbivore	_____ _____	vole
_____ _____	an animal that eats only other animals	great horned owl
_____ _____	an animal that eats both plants and animals	_____ _____

C. Replace the underlined words and phrases to tell how energy is used by different links in the food chain.

1. A food chain shows the path of food energy in an ecosystem from <u>animals to plants</u>.

_____

2. A plant gets energy from <u>other plants</u>.

_____

3. An herbivore gets food energy from <u>the Sun</u>.

_____

4. A predator gets <u>prey</u> from the plants that were eaten by another animal.

_____

5. Each link in a food chain uses <u>force</u> to grow and live.

_____

What Are Food Webs?

> carnivore   food chain   herbivore
> omnivore   photosynthesis

Use the words from the box to complete the diagram about how living things get energy.

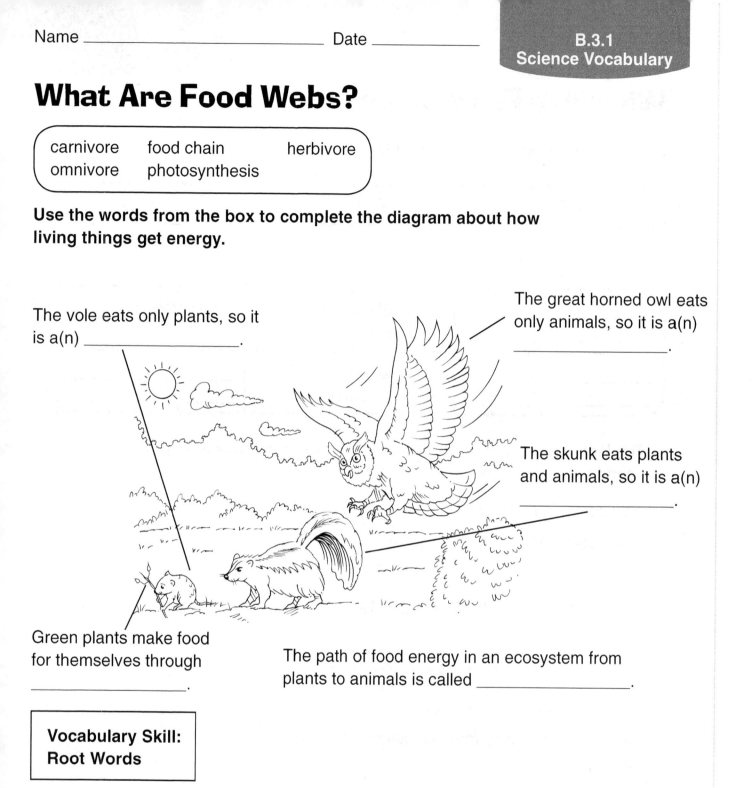

The vole eats only plants, so it is a(n) _____.

The great horned owl eats only animals, so it is a(n) _____.

The skunk eats plants and animals, so it is a(n) _____.

Green plants make food for themselves through _____.

The path of food energy in an ecosystem from plants to animals is called _____.

**Vocabulary Skill:
Root Words**

The Greek root *photo* can mean "radiant energy," and the Greek root *syntithenai* means "to put together." Combine the meaning of these root words to write your own definition of *photosynthesis*.

_____

_____

Use with pages 86–93

What Are Food Chains?

Glossary

consumer	an organism that eats plants or animals for food
ecosystem	all the living and nonliving things in a certain area
predator	an animal that lives by hunting other animals for food
prey	an animal that is hunted by another animal for food
producer	an organism that makes its own food

Use a word from the box to rewrite each sentence to make it true.

1. Mice are predators of great horned owls.

_____

_____

2. In a pond ecosystem, tiny plants are examples of consumers.

_____

_____

3. An area in which animals and plants live alongside nonliving things is called a food chain.

_____

_____

4. In a food chain, animals are examples of producers.

_____

_____

5. An ecosystem is an animal that hunts other animals for food.

_____

_____

Homework: Write two or three sentences explaining how one animal can be a predator as well as prey.

What Are Food Webs?

Main Idea In an ecosystem, overlapping food chains form food webs.

- In every kind of ecosystem, energy enters food webs through plants and plantlike organisms.

- Some plants and animals link together in many overlapping food chains to make a food web.

- Many organisms, from tiny algae to giant whales, form overlapping food chains to make up an ocean food web.

A. Replace the underlined words and phrases to tell about ecosystems.

Only plants _____ exist in ecosystems.

Most ecosystems contain one type of plant or animal _____

_____. These plants and animals form

microorganisms _____. At the start of every food chain,

energy enters through bacteria _____.

When two or more ecosystems _____ overlap, they form

a food web.

B. Put a check next to the statements about food chains and food webs that are true.

_____ A plant can be part of only one food chain.

_____ Each plant or animal in an ecosystem is part of more than one food chain.

_____ Food chains and food webs are different in different ecosystems.

_____ A predator may be part of more than one food chain.

_____ When two food chains overlap, they form a food web.

_____ In a food web, at least two plants and three animals are part of another food chain.

What Are Food Webs?

C. Study the chart of an ocean food web. Then answer the questions below.

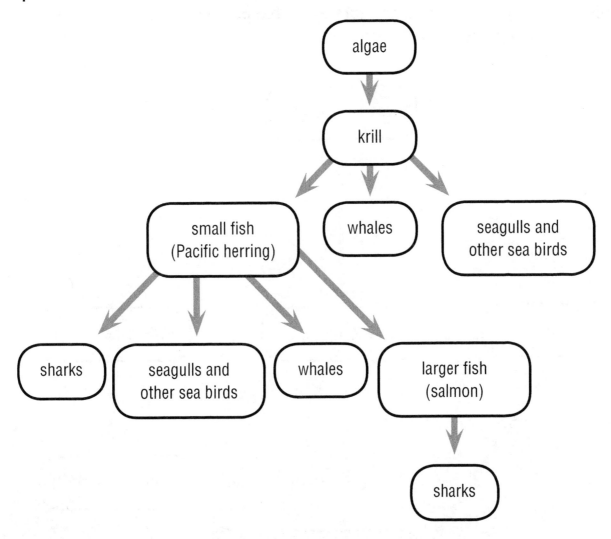

1. What is the largest organism in the ocean food web shown above? _____

2. What is the smallest organism in the ocean food web shown above? _____

3. According to the diagram, which organisms are definitely part of more than one food chain? _____

_____

What Are Food Webs?

food web

Complete the diagram by shading rectangles that contain an example of overlapping food chains.

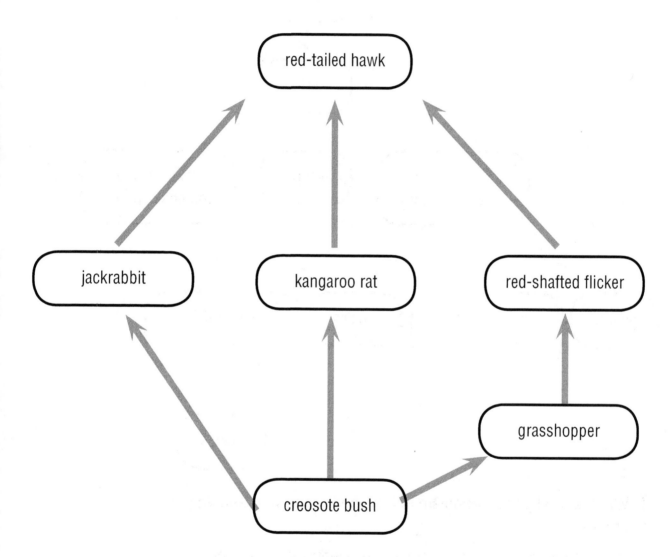

Homework: Write one or two sentences to explain the difference between a food web and a food chain. Then draw a diagram to illustrate how overlapping food chains form a food web.

Study Guide
36
Use with pages 94–99

What Are Food Webs?

Glossary

animal	a living thing that takes in food and moves about
ecosystem	all the living and nonliving things in a certain area
food chain	a group of living things that form a chain in which the first living thing is eaten by the second, the second by the third, and so on
plant	a living thing that stays in one place and makes its own food

Use a word from the box to rewrite each sentence about food webs to make it true.

1. A food web contains everything—living and nonliving—in a particular place.

   _____

   _____

2. A creosote bush is an example of an insect that is one part of a desert food web.

   _____

   _____

3. Overlapping environments form a food web.

   _____

   _____

4. Flickers, hawks, jackrabbits, and kangaroo rats are examples of predators that live in a desert landscape.

   _____

   _____

What Are Microorganisms?

Main Idea Microorganisms are an important and necessary part of most ecosystems. Many kinds of microorganisms are helpful in making food. Others form the basis of food chains in oceans.

- Bacteria in your body are microorganisms that help you digest and get nutrients from food.

- Microorganisms help in the process of making certain foods.

- Microorganisms in the ocean use the Sun's energy to make food, and they produce most of the world's oxygen.

A. Complete the diagram to tell about the functions of bacteria.

What Are Microorganisms?

B. Complete the diagrams to tell about how bacteria change the properties of foods.

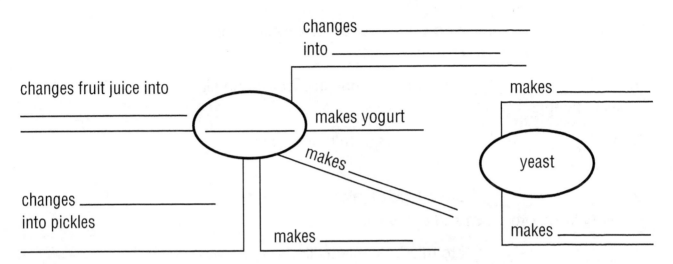

changes _____
into _____

changes fruit juice into
_____

makes _____

makes yogurt

makes _____

yeast

changes _____
into pickles

makes _____

makes _____

makes _____

C. Complete the diagram to tell about microorganisms in the ocean.

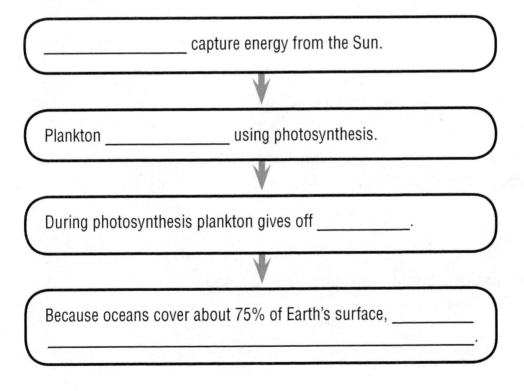

_____ capture energy from the Sun.

Plankton _____ using photosynthesis.

During photosynthesis plankton gives off _____.

Because oceans cover about 75% of Earth's surface, _____
_____.

Study Guide

39

Use with pages 102–107

What Are Microorganisms?

> bacteria   cell
> microorganism   plankton

Use the words in the box to complete each sentence. Some words may be used more than once.

1. A _____ is the basic unit that makes up all living things.

2. A _____ is an organism that cannot be seen without a microscope.

3. _____ are a type of microorganism found in every living organism and everywhere on Earth.

4. _____ are microorganisms that live in water.

5. Some simple organisms consist of only one _____.

6. Some _____ cause illness, such as strep throat and Lyme disease.

7. Yeast is a kind of _____.

8. _____ form an invisible film over all of Earth's oceans.

9. Without the helpful _____ that live in your body, you would not be able to digest food.

10. Many kinds of _____ are microscopic plants or one-celled algae.

Homework: Write a paragraph that explains the positive and negative aspects of bacteria.

What Are Microorganisms?

Glossary

energy	the capacity for doing work
invisible	not able to be seen
microscopic	so small it can be seen only through a microscope
plentiful	more than enough
process	a series of actions performed in making or doing something

Use the words in the box to complete the diagram by telling about plankton.

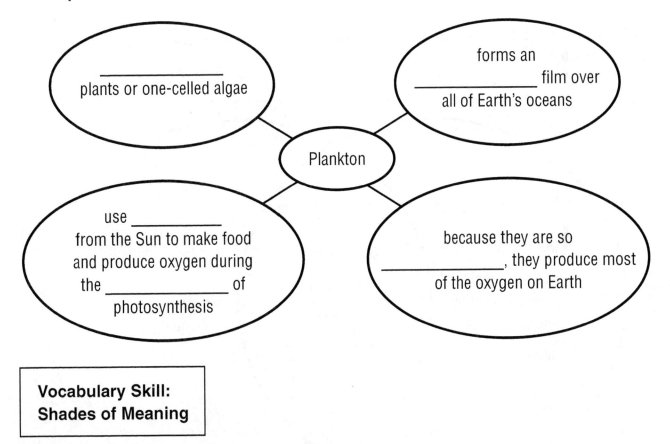

_____
plants or one-celled algae

forms an
_____ film over
all of Earth's oceans

Plankton

use _____
from the Sun to make food
and produce oxygen during
the _____ of
photosynthesis

because they are so
_____, they produce most
of the oxygen on Earth

**Vocabulary Skill:
Shades of Meaning**

Explain how to distinguish between the meanings of the words *microscopic* and *invisible*.

_____

_____

_____

How Is Matter Cycled in an Ecosystem?

Main Idea Organisms such as scavengers and decomposers recycle matter from dead plants and animals. They turn this matter into a form that can be used by other organisms.

- Scavengers are consumers that get energy from the remains of dead organisms.

- Decomposers help decay, or break down, the remains of dead organisms.

- People can create an ideal environment for decomposers by making a compost pile or bin.

A. Complete the diagram to compare and contrast scavengers and predators.

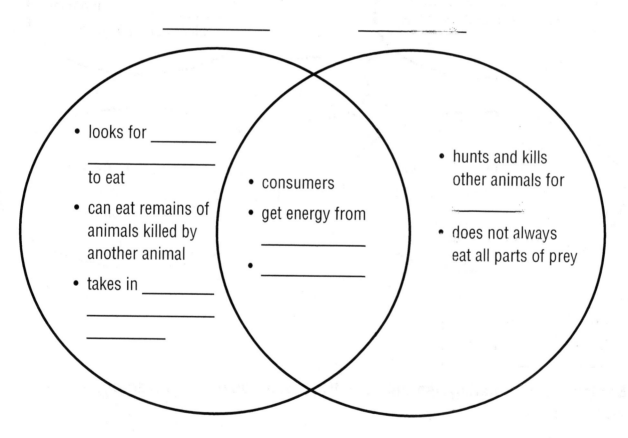

- looks for _____

_____ to eat

- can eat remains of animals killed by another animal

- takes in _____

_____

_____

- consumers

- get energy from

_____

- _____

- hunts and kills other animals for

_____

- does not always eat all parts of prey

Name _____ Date _____

How Is Matter Cycled in an Ecosystem?

B. Complete the diagram by providing details about decomposers.

Fungi are a group of
organisms that include

_____.

Ants, termites, worms, and beetles help the
process of _____ by making

_____

Fungi such as mushrooms and mold _____
that help break down dead plants.

C. Put a check next to the reasons why the process of decomposing and recycling materials from organic matter is important to an ecosystem.

_____ Decomposers help new plants grow by helping wood
logs decay.

_____ Nutrients released by bacteria from dead plants and animals
enrich the soil.

_____ A fallen tree can provide food and shelter for decomposers,
scavengers, producers, herbivores, and carnivores.

_____ Decomposers keep the environment from becoming filled
with the remains of dead plants and animals.

_____ Some types of bacteria cause disease, and mold can cause
foods to spoil.

Use with pages 118–125

How Is Matter Cycled in an Ecosystem?

compost   decay   scavenger
decomposer nutrient recycling

Use the words from the box to complete the sentences about the cycling of matter in an ecosystem.

1. When something _____, it breaks down into simpler materials.

2. A _____ is an animal that feeds on the remains or wastes of dead animals.

3. A _____ is a living thing that breaks down the remains of dead organisms.

4. Decayed material from once-living things, called _____, is used to enrich soil.

5. _____ is the process of breaking down materials into a different form that can be used again.

Homework: Make a list of six scavengers and six decomposers. Then illustrate and label one example of each.

How Is Matter Cycled in an Ecosystem?

Glossary

available	ready for use and service
encourage	to give help to or help bring about
enrich	to improve or make better by adding something
environment	the air, the water, the soil, and all the other things that surround a person, animal or plant
ideal	perfect
release	to set free

Use the words from the box to complete the paragraphs about composting.

Decomposers _____ nutrients that other organisms need to survive. Also, decomposers free up living space in the _____. As dead plants and animals decay, the space they took up becomes _____ to other living things.

By creating _____ conditions, people can _____ decomposers to grow. One way of doing this is to make a place where natural materials can become compost. Compost can be returned to the soil to _____ it.

**Vocabulary Skill:
Multiple-Meaning Words**

Some words have more than one meaning. For example, one meaning of the verb *release* is "to set free." The word can also be used to mean "to allow to be seen, published, or broadcast." Which meaning of *release* is intended in this sentence?

Bacteria release nutrients into the soil by breaking down dead plants and animals.

_____

_____

How Do People Affect Ecosystems?

Main Idea Like other organisms, people change the ecosystems in which they live. Human changes to an ecosystem can affect the ability of other organisms to survive in those ecosystems.

- People clear forests, and forest plants and animals lose their habitat and don't survive.

- People harm organisms by polluting land ecosystems and damming rivers.

- Pollution of water ecosystems causes danger to people and other organisms.

A. Complete the diagram to tell how humans can affect a forest habitat.

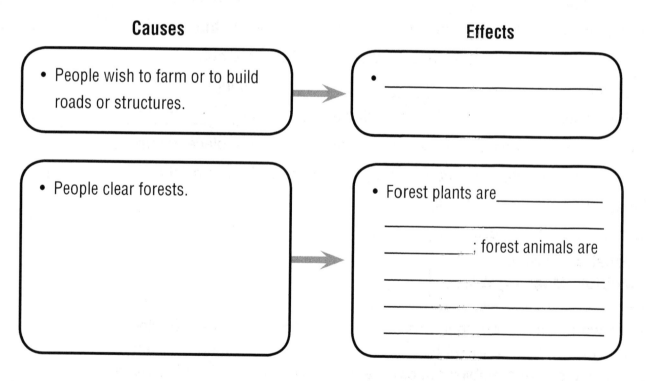

Causes

- People wish to farm or to build roads or structures.

- People clear forests.

Effects

- _____

- Forest plants are_____
  _____
  _____; forest animals are
  _____
  _____
  _____

How Do People Affect Ecosystems?

B. Complete the diagram to tell about things that are harmful to land ecosystems.

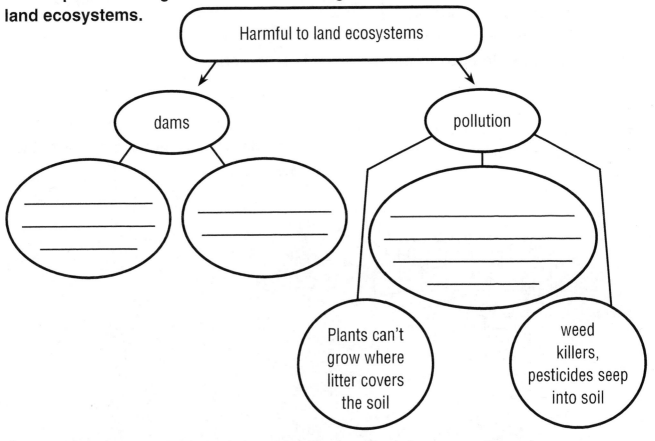

Harmful to land ecosystems

dams

pollution

Plants can't grow where litter covers the soil

weed killers, pesticides seep into soil

C. Rewrite each statement about the effects of wastes on water ecosystems to make it true.

1. When people dispose of waste products properly, pollution to water ecosystems can result.

   _____

   _____

2. Harmless wastes include motor oil, paint, insect sprays, and many cleaning supplies.

   _____

   _____

3. Hazardous wastes rarely are a danger to organisms.

   _____

   _____

Use with pages 128–133

Name _____ Date _____

How Do People Affect Ecosystems?

> hazardous waste   litter
> pollutant   pollution

Use the words in the box to complete each sentence.

One common _____ on land
is _____—that is, trash that is
disposed of in a way that causes harm
to ecosystems.

The addition of harmful materials to the
environment is called _____.

Waste that can pollute the environment even when it occurs in very small
amounts is known as a _____.

Homework: Think about a place in your town or city that is affected
by pollution. Write a few sentences describing the type of pollution
that exists, as well as your ideas on how to clean up the harmful
materials.

Use with pages 128–133

How Do People Affect Ecosystems?

Glossary

harmful	bad for one's health; dangerous
provide	to give what is needed or wanted
replace	to take or fill the place of
survive	to continue to exist
technology	methods, machines, and devices that are used in doing things in a science or profession

Use the words from the box to complete the sentences about land ecosystems.

1. When people clear forest land for farming, crop plants and farm animals _____ forest plants and forest animals.

2. People sometimes add _____ materials to ecosystems.

3. People can use _____ to change a forest into a city.

4. Dams are built to control flooding, bring water to dry areas to grow crops, and _____ water for people in cities.

5. Often the living things in these places cannot _____ once the places are changed for human use.

Homework: Write two or three sentences describing changes you have observed to land in your neighborhood or community. How have people in your community affected the ecosystem?

How Can Ecosystems Be Conserved?

Main Idea Some of the ways ecosystems can be conserved include using biodegradable materials, recycling, and practicing green agriculture.

- Biodegradable materials are broken down in the environment by microorganisms.

- Waste materials cannot break down in landfills. Zero waste practices can help conserve ecosystems.

- Green agriculture involves farming methods that do not harm ecosystems.

A. Complete the diagrams to tell about biodegradable materials.

How Can Ecosystems Be Conserved?

B. Rewrite each statement about landfills and zero waste practices to make it true.

1. The garbage in a landfill is packed so tightly that microorganisms that break down waste materials can survive there.

_____

_____

_____

2. The goal of zero waste is to make and use as much natural and manufactured materials as possible.

_____

_____

_____

C. Complete the outline to describe green agriculture.

I. Green agriculture employs farming methods that

_____.

  A. Organic farmers use only materials that _____

_____

    1. Organic farmers avoid _____

_____.

  B. Crop rotation involves growing a different crop on a field each year.

    1. Only small amounts of different nutrients are _____

_____.

    2. Farmers use much less _____.

  C. Green farmers also grow cover crops.

    1. Cover crops are _____

    2. They conserve _____, control _____, and provide _____

How Can Ecosystems Be Conserved?

biodegradable material   ecotourism

Use the words from the box to complete the following chart.

	What It Is	How It Helps Environment
_____ _____	matter that is broken down easily by microorganisms	• saves space in landfills • prevents trash from causing pollution
_____ _____	careful, responsible travel to natural habitats	• provides income for people living there • avoids harming natural habitats • helps preserve areas and organisms living there • encourages more people to help preserve natural habitats

**Vocabulary Skill:
Prefixes**

The word *ecotourism* contains the prefix *eco-*. What is the meaning
of this prefix? What other words have you read that contain this prefix?

_____

_____

How Can Ecosystems Be Conserved?

Glossary

climate	the average weather conditions of a place or region throughout the year
disasters	events that cause much suffering or loss
drought	a long period of time with little or no rain
flood	a great flow of water over normally dry land
hurricane	a storm with very strong winds and heavy rain

Use the words from the box to complete the diagram and tell about the effects of destroying the rainforests.

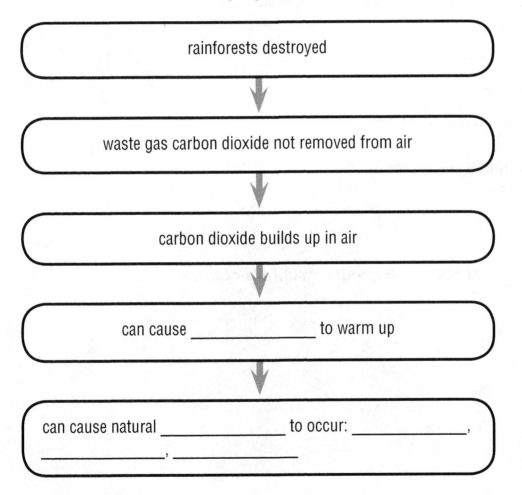

rainforests destroyed

waste gas carbon dioxide not removed from air

carbon dioxide builds up in air

can cause _____ to warm up

can cause natural _____ to occur: _____, _____, _____

Homework: Write one or two sentences that describe the important role that rainforests play in providing oxygen for living things on Earth.

Use with pages 134–143

What Are the Properties of Minerals?

Main Idea Minerals can be described according to a set of properties including luster, color, streak, hardness, and cleavage.

- Luster is the way a mineral shines, or reflects light.
- The color of a mineral depends on its chemical makeup.
- The hardness of a mineral is a measure of how easily the mineral can be scratched.
- Cleavage is the tendency of a mineral to split easily along flat surfaces.

A. Put a check next to each property of a mineral.

_____ nonliving solid

_____ definite chemical makeup

_____ made up of cells

_____ found in Earth's outermost layer

B. Explain what a mineral's luster is.

_____

_____

C. Complete each sentence to tell about a mineral's color.

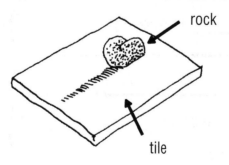

rock

tile

The color of this mineral depends on its _____.

The color of this mineral when it is ground to a powder is called its _____.

What Are the Properties of Minerals?

D. Fill in the blanks to describe the hardness of minerals.

The _____ of a mineral is a measure of how easily a mineral can be scratched. You can test for the property of hardness by using different objects to _____ the mineral.

Another way to test hardness is to compare a mineral to the minerals listed in the _____. There are _____ minerals on the scale. _____ is number 1 and the softest mineral. _____ is number 10 and the hardest mineral.

Like all matter, minerals are made of tiny particles. The way in which a mineral's particles are _____ determines the hardness of the mineral.

E. Use the following words in a sentence to tell about cleavage.

1. cleavage

_____

_____

2. cleavage planes

_____

_____

3. facets

_____

_____

Name _____ Date _____

What Are the Properties of Minerals?

cleavage   hardness   luster
mineral   streak

A. Complete the chart to show the properties of minerals.

Mineral Properties

Property Name	Description
_____	color of a mineral when it is ground to a powder
_____	the way a mineral reflects light
_____	the tendency of a mineral to split easily along flat surfaces
_____	a measure of how easily the mineral can be scratched

B. Write a paragraph that describes what a mineral is. Give two examples of how minerals are used.

_____

_____

_____

_____

_____

_____

What Are the Properties of Minerals?

Glossary

facets	the flat polished surfaces cut on a gemstone
impurities	substances that adulterate or contaminate something
makeup	the way in which something is composed or arranged
particles	very small pieces of something
properties	characteristics or traits

A. Use the words from the box to complete each sentence.

1. A mineral is a nonliving solid material that has a definite chemical

   _____.

2. The _____ of minerals make them useful in
   many ways.

3. _____ in a mineral can affect its color.

4. Like all matter, minerals are made of tiny _____.

5. Gemcutters grind some minerals to produce shiny, sparkling
   surfaces that reflect light, called _____.

**B. Each statement describes a mineral. Put a check next to each
description that is a property of the mineral.**

_____ **1.** Sunscreen is made from zincite.

_____ **2.** Diamond is the hardest mineral.

_____ **3.** Talcum powder is made with talc.

_____ **4.** Aluminum is made from bauxite.

_____ **5.** Azurite is deep blue.

_____ **6.** The mineral fluorite has a glassy luster.

How Are Minerals Identified?

Main Idea The properties of a mineral can be determined by observing and by carrying out a series of tests. Then, by comparing its properties with those listed in a table of mineral properties, the mineral can be identified.

- You can use the mineral properties listed in a table to identify an unknown mineral.

- A nonmetallic mineral is dull or glassy.

- A metallic mineral is shiny like a metal.

A. Complete the diagram to show how to classify a mineral's luster.

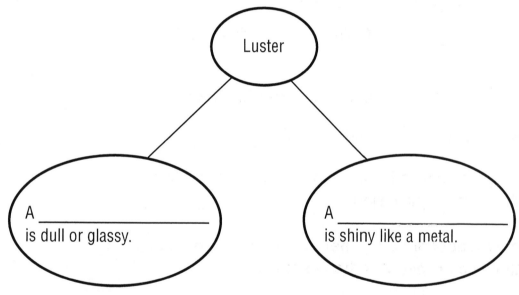

Luster

A _____
is dull or glassy.

A _____
is shiny like a metal.

B. Number the events below to show the order you would follow to identify an unknown mineral using the Properties of Minerals table.

_____ Test for hardness to find out what scratches the mineral.

_____ Compare the color of the mineral with the colors listed in the table.

_____ Find out what special properties your mineral has.

_____ Use luster to find out if the mineral is nonmetallic or metallic.

How Are Minerals Identified?

C. Answer the questions to tell how to identify unknown minerals.

1. What table can you use to identify an unknown mineral?

   _____

2. How can you tell if a mineral is a nonmetallic mineral?

   _____

3. How can you tell if a mineral is a metallic mineral?

   _____

4. What mineral property are you testing if a fingernail scratches a mineral?

   _____

5. What mineral property are you testing if a mineral splits along a flat surface?

   _____

6. What mineral property are you testing if you scratch a mineral on a ceramic tile?

   _____

7. What are some other properties a mineral might have?

   _____

How Are Minerals Identified?

metallic mineral   nonmetallic mineral

Complete the diagram to compare and contrast a metallic mineral and a nonmetallic mineral. Then write an example of each mineral.

_____   _____

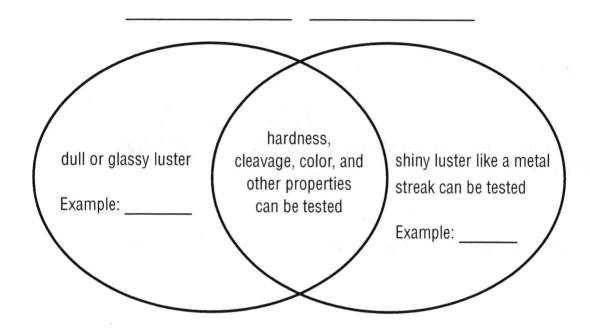

dull or glassy luster

Example: _____

hardness, cleavage, color, and other properties can be tested

shiny luster like a metal streak can be tested

Example: _____

Homework: Write a short paragraph explaining how you can test whether a mineral is metallic or nonmetallic.

How Are Minerals Identified?

Glossary

dull	does not reflect light; not shiny
glassy	reflects light like glass
flat	having a smooth, level surface
shiny	reflects light; bright
ceramic	made of pottery or porcelain
magnetic	attracts iron objects

Match one or more of the adjectives from the box with what it can be used to describe.

1. a metallic mineral's luster

_____

2. a metallic mineral with a special property

_____

3. a nonmetallic mineral's luster

_____

4. a tile for testing streak

_____

5. a mineral's cleavage surface

_____

**Vocabulary Skill:
Antonyms**

Antonyms are words that have opposite meanings. Find two words in the box that are antonyms. Use each word in a sentence.

_____

_____

How Do Rocks Differ?

Main Idea Three basic kinds of rock—igneous, sedimentary, and metamorphic—make up Earth's crust. Each kind of rock forms in a different way and has different characteristics.

- Igneous rock forms when molten rock cools and hardens.

- Sedimentary rock forms when sand, particles of rock, bits of soil, and remains of once-living things are pressed together and harden.

- Metamorphic rock forms when existing rocks are changed by heat, pressure, or chemicals beneath Earth's surface.

A. Complete each sentence to tell about the layers of Earth.

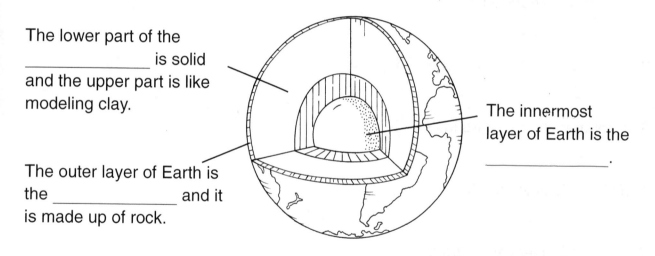

The lower part of the _____ is solid and the upper part is like modeling clay.

The outer layer of Earth is the _____ and it is made up of rock.

The innermost layer of Earth is the _____.

B. Complete the diagram to tell how igneous rock forms.

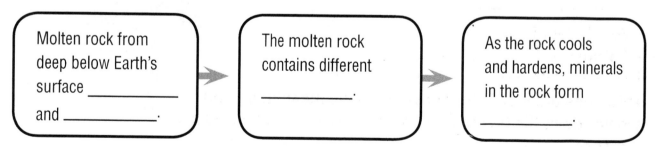

Molten rock from deep below Earth's surface _____ and _____.

The molten rock contains different _____.

As the rock cools and hardens, minerals in the rock form _____.

How Do Rocks Differ?

C. Number the events to show how sedimentary rocks form.

_____ Dissolved minerals fill in any cracks and cement, or glue, all of the particles together.

_____ Sediment is carried by wind, moving water, and moving ice.

_____ Rock is broken into sediment by natural forces in a process called weathering.

_____ Layers of sediment are deposited on top of one another.

_____ As the layers build up, their weight produces more and more pressure on the bottom layers.

D. Complete the paragraphs to describe how metamorphic rocks form.

New rock that forms when existing rocks are changed by

heat, pressure, or chemicals beneath Earth's surface is called

_____. Both _____and sedimentary

rock can be changed into metamorphic rock.

Rocks are under great _____ beneath Earth's

surface. The pressure causes _____ to build up, which

causes the rocks to change.

If you look closely at samples of metamorphic rock, you'll notice

that some of the _____ in the rock are flattened.

This is due to the great _____ that formed the rock.

Examples of metamorphic rock include gneiss, _____,

and _____.

How Do Rocks Differ?

igneous rock   rock   sedimentary rock
metamorphic rock   sediment

A. Use the words from the box to complete the diagram about the three basic kinds of rocks.

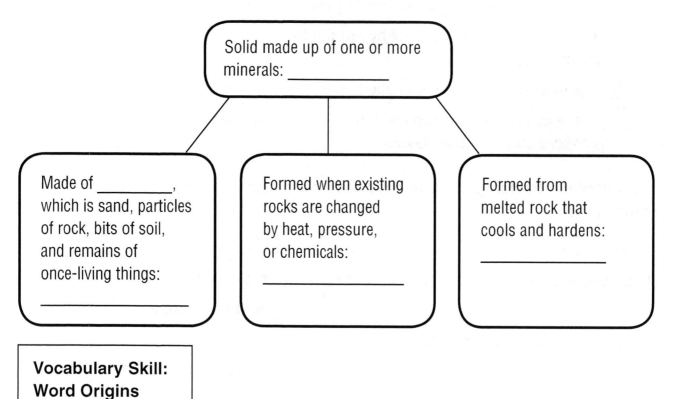

Solid made up of one or more minerals: _____

Made of _____, which is sand, particles of rock, bits of soil, and remains of once-living things:

_____

Formed when existing rocks are changed by heat, pressure, or chemicals:

_____

Formed from melted rock that cools and hardens:

_____

**Vocabulary Skill:
Word Origins**

B. The word *igneous* comes from a Latin word that means "fire,"and the word *sedimentary* comes from a Latin word that means "to sit." Explain what the origin of each word tells about how igneous rock and sedimentary rock form.

_____

_____

_____

_____

How Do Rocks Differ?

Glossary

crystals	solids in which the atoms or molecules are arranged in a definite pattern
grains	tiny individual pieces of something
molten	changed into liquid form by heat
pressure	the applying of a firm regular weight or force against something
weathering	the disintegration and decomposition of rocks and minerals by natural processes

Use the words from the box to complete the chart about rocks found in Earth's crust.

Igneous	Igneous rock is rock that forms when melted, or _____, rock from deep below Earth's surface cools and hardens. The molten rock contains different minerals. As the rock cools and hardens, these minerals form _____. Igneous rocks can be classified by the size of their _____.
Sedimentary	Sedimentary rock is rock that forms when sand, particles of rock, bits of soil, and remains of once-living things are pressed together and harden. Rock is broken into sediment by natural forces in a process called _____ . As the layers of sediment build up, their weight produces more and more _____.
Metamorphic	Metamorphic rock is new rock that forms when existing rocks are changed by heat, _____, or chemicals beneath Earth's surface. If you look closely at samples of metamorphic rock, you'll notice that some of the _____ in the rock are flattened.

Study Guide
65
Use with pages 174–181

What Is the Rock Cycle?

Main Idea Any type of rock—metamorphic, igneous, or sedimentary—can change into any other type of rock. The continuous series of changes that rocks undergo is called the rock cycle.

- Heat and pressure can change igneous, sedimentary, and metamorphic rock into new metamorphic rock.

- Weathering is a process that changes rocks into sediment.

- Cementing is a process that changes sediments into sedimentary rock.

A. Sort the words below into two groups to show how rock can change into new rock. Some words may be used more than once.

heat	pressure	cementing
ice	wind	sediment
molten	hardens	weathering
cools	chemicals	water

words you could use to tell how metamorphic rock becomes sedimentary rock	words you could use to tell how metamorphic rock becomes igneous rock

Use with pages 184–189

What Is the Rock Cycle?

B. Complete the diagram to show how rocks change in the rock cycle.

The continuous series of changes that rocks undergo is the _____ .

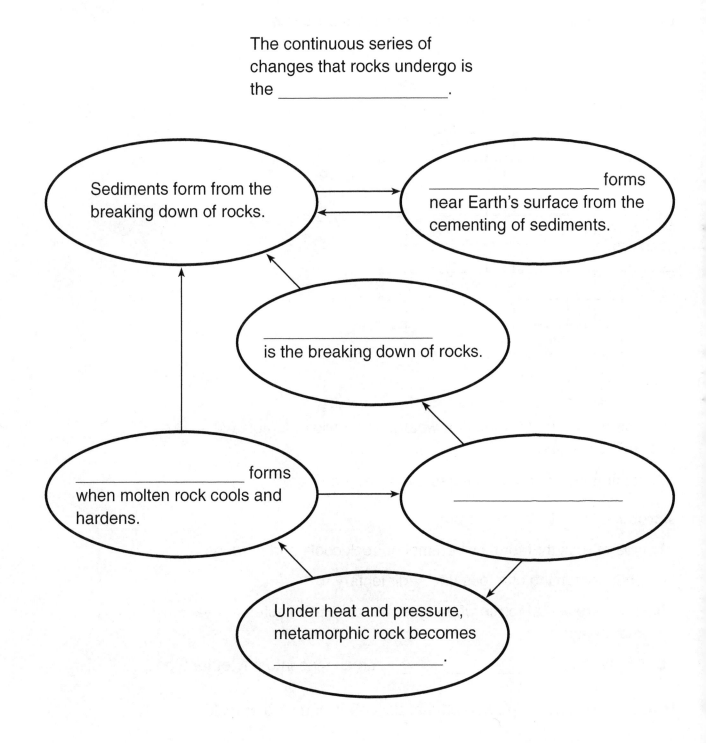

Sediments form from the breaking down of rocks.

_____ forms near Earth's surface from the cementing of sediments.

_____ is the breaking down of rocks.

_____ forms when molten rock cools and hardens.

_____

Under heat and pressure, metamorphic rock becomes _____ .

What Is the Rock Cycle?

| igneous rock | metamorphic rock | rock |
| rock cycle | sediment | sedimentary rock |

Use the words from the box to complete the puzzle.

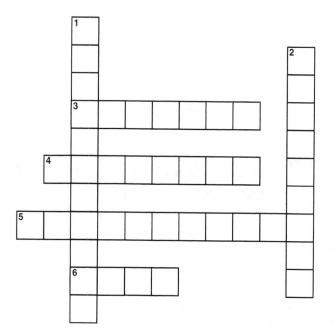

Down

1. type of rock that forms after weathering, building up of layers, and cementing

2. continuous series of changes that rocks undergo

Across

3. type of rock that forms when melted rock cools and hardens

4. what cementing changes into sedimentary rock

5. type of rock that forms when igneous rock is subjected to heat and pressure

6. Any type of _____ can change into any other type.

Homework: Write a paragraph that describes one type of rock.

What Is the Rock Cycle?

Glossary

continuous	going on without interruption or break
subject	to cause to undergo or experience
processes	series of actions, changes, or functions bringing about a result
sediment	material eroded from rocks by weathering
dissolved	broken up or disintegrated

Use the words from the box to complete the summary.

Any type of rock can change into any other type of rock. Scientists call

the _____ series of changes that rocks undergo the rock

cycle. The rock cycle shows the _____ that change rock.

For example, when heat and pressure are great enough, metamorphic

rocks become molten, or melted. When this melted rock cools and hardens,

it forms igneous rock. When igneous rock, in turn, is _____

to heat and pressure, it becomes metamorphic rock.

One way rocks can change is through the process of weathering.

It changes igneous, metamorphic, and sedimentary rocks into

_____.

Cementing is the process that changes sediments into sedimentary

rock. Over time, layers of sediment build up. Pressure from the

upper layers slowly changes the lower layers of sediment into rock.

_____ minerals fill in any cracks in the rock, cementing,

or gluing, the particles of sediment together.

Study Guide
69
Use with pages 184–189

Name _____ Date _____

What Are Earthquakes?

Main Idea Earth's surface is constantly changing. Earthquakes cause rapid changes to Earth's surface.

- Forces deep inside Earth put pressure on the rock layers above.

- An earthquake occurs when pressure on the rock layers becomes too great, and Earth's crust on one or both sides of a fault moves suddenly.

- Earthquakes occur when sections of Earth's crust come together, move apart, or slide past each other.

A. Complete the sentences to tell when and where earthquakes occur.

Earthquakes occur when sections of the crust come together, move apart, or

_____

each other.

Movements of the crust usually take place along a

_____ ,

or crack, in Earth's crust.

B. Number the events in order to tell how an earthquake occurs.

_____ The pressure builds up for hundreds or thousands of years.

_____ One or both sections on either side of the fault may move suddenly.

_____ The pressure on the rock layers becomes too great.

_____ An earthquake occurs.

_____ Forces deep inside Earth put pressure on the rock layers above.

Study Guide

70

What Are Earthquakes?

C. Rewrite each statement about earthquakes to make it true.

1. An earthquake that occurs in the ocean floor can sometimes cause a fault.

   _____

   _____

2. Seismologists measure the intensity of an earthquake using the Richter scale.

   _____

   _____

D. Check safety guidelines for staying safe during and after an earthquake.

Before an Earthquake:

_____ Use steel frames to reinforce homes and other buildings.

_____ Use brick and stone to build buildings.

During an Earthquake:

_____ Stay indoors and take cover near an inside wall.

_____ Turn lights on and off or use candles or matches.

_____ If you are in a car, stay there with your seatbelt fastened.

_____ If you are outdoors, find an area near a building and crouch down with your head covered.

After an Earthquake:

_____ Know which radio station to tune to.

_____ Use the telephone to call your family and friends to make sure they are OK.

Use with pages 198–205

What Are Earthquakes?

creep   earthquake   epicenter   fault
focus   seismology   tsunami

Use the words from the box to complete each sentence. Then circle each word in the puzzle.

n	e	w	e	y	b	l	l	c	t	f
x	p	d	g	j	n	p	r	s	b	a
z	i	m	h	x	f	a	u	l	t	h
b	c	r	e	e	p	c	k	s	i	q
s	e	i	s	m	o	l	o	g	y	v
i	n	f	t	f	q	c	b	b	x	l
j	t	s	u	n	a	m	i	w	d	r
e	e	a	r	t	h	q	u	a	k	e
k	r	d	w	q	l	a	z	o	g	r

1. Movements of the crust usually take place along a(n)

   _____.

2. The _____ is the point underground where an
   earthquake starts.

3. An earthquake can sometimes cause a(n) _____,
   a very large ocean wave.

4. The study of earthquakes is called _____.

5. A(n) _____ is a sudden movement of part of
   Earth's crust.

6. Slow movement along a fault is called _____.

7. The _____ is where an earthquake is felt
   most strongly.

What Are Earthquakes?

Glossary

brick	an oblong block baked until hard and used as a building and paving material
sometimes	now and then
steel	mixture of iron, carbon, and other metals
stone	rock
underground	located below Earth's surface
wood	trees cut and dried for use as building material and fuel

Use the words from the box to complete the paragraph about building design.

Buildings can be designed so they are less likely to collapse during

an earthquake. Materials such as _____ and _____

tend to crack and break when the ground beneath them shakes.

To withstand earthquakes, materials need to bend, or be flexible.

_____ and _____ are flexible. Buildings made with

these materials will move and sway but usually will not crack and fall.

**Vocabulary Skill:
Compound Word**

Tell how you can figure out the meaning of a compound word by thinking about the meanings of the two words in the compound word.

sometimes: _____

_____

_____

_____

underground: _____

_____

_____

_____

Study Guide

Use with pages 198–205

What Are Volcanoes?

Main Idea A volcano erupts when pressure pushes molten rock up through cracks in Earth's crust and onto the surface. Volcanoes change Earth's surface.

- A volcano is an opening in Earth's crust through which hot ash, gases, and molten rock escape from deep within Earth.

- Volcanoes can erupt in different ways.

- An erupting volcano can quickly change Earth's surface.

A. Complete the sentences to show how a volcano erupts.

A _____ is an opening in Earth's crust through which hot ash, gases, and molten rock escape from deep within Earth.

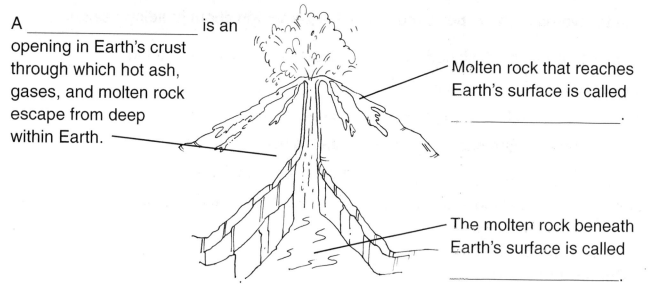

Molten rock that reaches Earth's surface is called

_____ .

The molten rock beneath Earth's surface is called

_____ .

B. Number the events below to show the order in which Mount St. Helens changed the landscape.

_____ When the eruption was over, the surrounding landscape was completely changed.

_____ In 1980, magma pushing upward caused Mount St. Helens to begin to erupt.

_____ Eruptions of gases, ash, and lava formed Mount St. Helens.

_____ The major eruption in May lasted for nine hours. Rock, mud, and water crashed down the mountain.

What Are Volcanoes?

C. Rewrite each sentence to make the statement about volcanoes true.

1. Volcanoes do not change Earth's surface.

_____

2. Deep within Earth's mantle, it is so cold in some places that rocks become frozen.

_____

_____

3. Pressure beneath the surface causes some magma to push its way through faults and flow onto Earth's surface as igneous rock.

_____

_____

_____

4. Mount St. Helens is a volcano that has existed since 1980.

_____

_____

D. Complete the chart to tell the different ways volcanoes erupt.

What Some Volcanoes Release	What Other Volcanoes Release

What Are Volcanoes?

lava   magma   volcano

Use the words from the box to complete the diagram to tell about volcanoes.

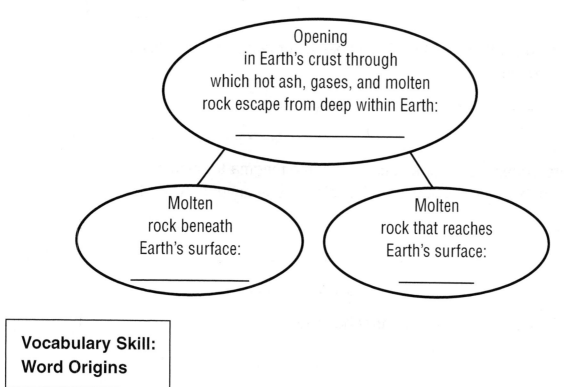

Opening
in Earth's crust through
which hot ash, gases, and molten
rock escape from deep within Earth:

_____

Molten
rock beneath
Earth's surface:

_____

Molten
rock that reaches
Earth's surface:

_____

Vocabulary Skill:
Word Origins

The word *volcano* comes from the name for the Roman god of fire, Vulcan. Explain what the origin of the word tells about its meaning.

_____

_____

_____

What are Volcanoes?

Glossary

erupt	to force out or release violently
escape	to get free
push	to exert force against
release	to set free or let go
rise	to move from a lower to a higher position
spew	to send or force out as if in a stream

Use the words to complete the sentences about volcanoes.

1. Pressure beneath the surface causes some magna to

   _____ its way through faults and flow onto

   Earth's surface.

2. Some volcanoes _____ hot lava, ash,

   and gases into the air.

3. A volcano is an opening through which hot ash, gases, and

   molten rock _____ from deep within Earth.

4. Some volcanoes _____ thick, slow-moving lava.

5. Magma pushing upward caused Mount St. Helens to begin to

   _____.

6. As magma _____ to the surface, some of it

   slowly hardens and becomes igneous rock.

Homework: Write one sentence using three words from the box.

What Are Landslides?

Main Idea Landslides cause rapid changes to Earth's surface. There are many causes of landslides, including heavy rains, melting snow, earthquakes, and volcanic eruptions.

- A landslide is the sudden movement of loose rock and soil down a steep slope.

- Landslides can be very destructive.

- There are different types of landslides, including mudslides and rockslides.

A. Put a check next to each cause of a landslide.

_____ building hillside homes

_____ wildfires

_____ earthquakes

_____ heavy rains

_____ planting trees

_____ melting snow

B. Complete the diagram to tell about the destructive effects of landslides and how these effects can be reduced.

Effects of Landslides

Landslides can be destructive
in places where people have built
houses on _____
_____.
Every year landslides cause millions
of dollars in _____.

What Can Be Done to Reduce Effects

- local governments can
_____
_____

- supporting walls can be built to
_____

- people can consult with
_____

What Are Landslides?

C. Complete the diagram to compare and contrast mudslides and rockslides.

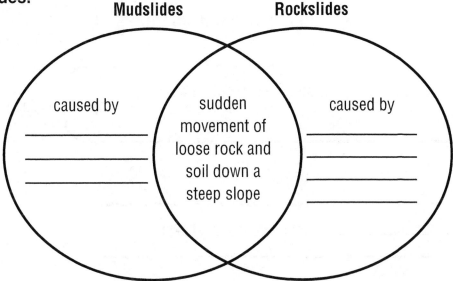

D. Complete the paragraph to tell about landslides.

_____ or volcanic eruptions can trigger landslides.

Soil and rock that have been loosened by the _____

land will slide downhill. The steeper the slope, the _____

materials will move downhill in a landslide. Without _____

to hold soil in place, the sudden movement of rocks and soil down the slope

is more likely.

What Are Landslides?

> earthquake   landslide   rock

Use the words in the box to complete the diagram.

A(n) _____, or sudden movement of part of Earth's crust, occurs.

↓

Soil and _____ are loosened by shaking.

↓

A(n) _____, or sudden movement of loose rock and soil down a steep slope, occurs.

**Vocabulary Skill:
Compound Words**

Tell how you can figure out the meaning of a compound word by thinking about the meaning of the two words in the compound word.

landslide: _____

_____

_____

_____

_____

_____

Study Guide

Use with pages 216–221

What Are Landslides?

Glossary

destructive	causing destruction
heavy	having great weight
loose	not tightly fastened or secured
massive	bulky, heavy, and solid
steep	sharply sloped
sudden	happening without warning

Use the words from the box to complete the story about a landslide.

On such a beautiful day, nobody expected trouble. But when the volcano erupted, it caused a _____ landslide to occur. Without warning, a _____ movement of _____ rock and soil down the slope took place.

The landslide was especially _____ at the beach where it crushed houses on hillsides and near the edge of _____ cliffs. Here the soil was wet, and a large, _____ mass of soil slid down. Many houses were destroyed, and millions of dollars in damage to property occurred.

Homework: Rewrite the story about a landslide as a news report to tell it. Use as many of the words from the box as you can.

Name _____ Date _____

What Are Weathering and Erosion?

Main Idea Earth's surface is slowly built up and worn down. The processes of weathering and erosion change Earth's surface.

- Weathering is the slow wearing away of rock into smaller pieces.
- Ice, plant roots, moving water, and chemicals cause weathering.
- Erosion is the movement of rock material from one place to another.
- Water, wind, and glaciers cause erosion.

A. Complete the diagram to compare and contrast erosion and weathering.

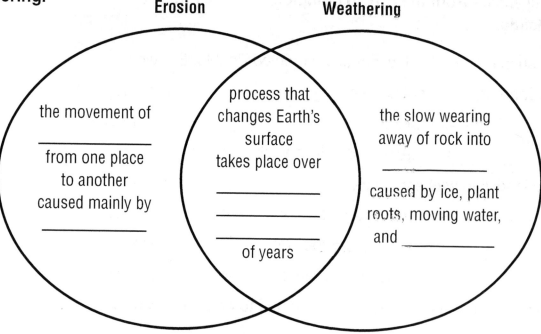

Erosion   Weathering

the movement of
_____
from one place
to another
caused mainly by
_____

process that changes Earth's surface takes place over
_____
_____
_____
of years

the slow wearing away of rock into
_____
caused by ice, plant roots, moving water, and _____

B. Number the events below to show the order in which weathering occurs.

_____ Over time, periods of freezing and melting cause the rocks to break.

_____ The expanding ice makes the cracks bigger.

_____ Rainwater freezes and expands.

_____ Rainwater enters cracks in rocks.

What Are Weathering and Erosion?

C. Complete the outline to describe weathering and erosion.

I. _____ is the slow wearing away of rock into smaller pieces.

   A. Rainwater that enters cracks can freeze and _____; periods of freezing and _____ cause rocks to break.

   B. Growing _____ widen cracks and the rock breaks.

   C. _____ flow over rocks, moving them. Over and over rocks bump against each other and get _____.

   D. Outer layers of rock can peel off when a(n) _____ or the Sun heats up the outside of a rock.

   E. When cool _____ falls on heated rocks, it can cause them to break.

   F. _____ can weather rocks.

      1. Gases in the air react with iron in some rocks to form _____, which crumbles.

      2. _____ weakens rock, causing it to break apart.

II. _____ is the movement of rock material from one place to another.

   A. _____ is the main cause of erosion.

   B. A(n) _____ is a large mass of slow-moving ice that causes erosion.

   C. _____ carries away dry sand and soil.

What Are Weathering and Erosion?

erosion   glacier   weathering

A. Think about how the words in the box are related. Then write each word where it belongs in the diagram.

_____ is the slow wearing away of rock into smaller pieces.

The materials that result from weathering are carried away by _____, the movement of rock material from one place to another.

One way rock material is moved is by a(n) _____, a large mass of slow-moving ice.

B. Explain how erosion is different from weathering.

_____

_____

_____

_____

What Are Weathering and Erosion?

Glossary

downhill	down the slopes of a steep hill
outside	on or to the external side
rainstorm	a storm with precipitation in the form of rain
rainwater	water that falls as rain

Use the compound words from the box to complete the puzzle.

Across

1. After a heavy _____, soil and pebbles can be carried away by running water.

Down

1. When cool _____ falls on heated rocks, it can cause them to break.
2. When water moves _____, it can pick up tiny particles.
3. Outer layers of rock can peel off when a forest fire or the Sun heats up the _____ of a rock.

> **Vocabulary Skill:**
> **Multiple-Meaning Words**

The words *figure* and *periods* have more than one meaning. Write another meaning for each word other than the one used in the sentence.

1. Acid rain has damaged this stone figure on a building in Paris, France.

_____

_____

2. Over time, periods of freezing and melting cause rocks to break.

_____

_____

How Does Water Shape the Land?

Main Idea Moving water changes Earth's surface through weathering, erosion, and deposition.

- Wind, glaciers, and moving water are the main causes of deposition.

- Deposition helps create a variety of land surface features.

- People can shape the land.

A. Complete the diagram to tell about the features created by deposition.

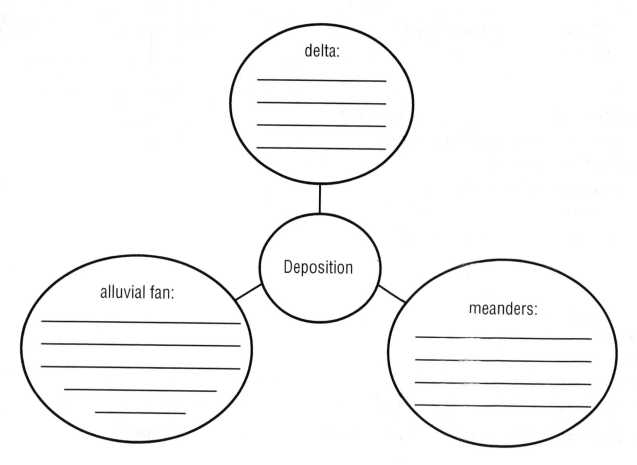

How Does Water Shape the Land?

B. Complete the graphic organizer to tell about a river system.

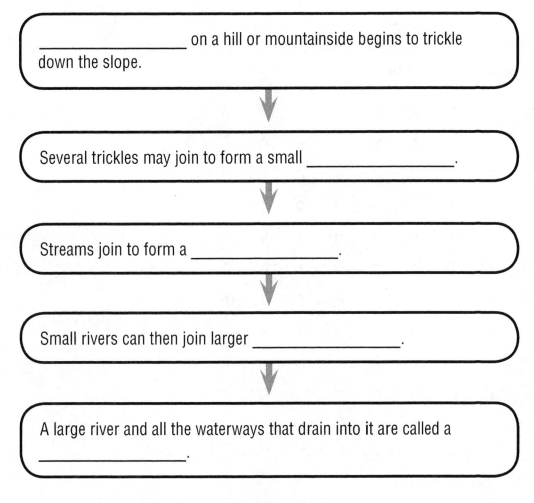

_____ on a hill or mountainside begins to trickle down the slope.

Several trickles may join to form a small _____.

Streams join to form a _____.

Small rivers can then join larger _____.

A large river and all the waterways that drain into it are called a _____.

C. Describe one way people shape the land.

_____

_____

_____

Use with pages 236–243

How Does Water Shape the Land?

bay   deposition   river system
delta   headland

Use the words from the box to complete each sentence. Then circle each word in the puzzle.

q	j	n	t	a	t	s	c	d	u	q
w	f	e	t	r	z	y	f	e	o	t
t	c	l	b	s	n	b	c	p	x	c
h	e	a	d	l	a	n	d	o	j	d
d	t	r	v	x	m	n	g	s	v	w
i	g	m	s	t	h	q	c	i	k	p
r	i	v	e	r	s	y	s	t	e	m
r	y	d	j	o	a	s	g	i	r	g
m	p	h	f	b	s	j	v	o	z	c
a	x	b	r	c	q	d	o	n	b	h

1. A _____ is a point of land, usually high, that
   extends out into the water.

2. A _____ is a body of water that is partly
   enclosed by land and has a wide opening.

3. A large river and all the waterways that drain into it are called
   a _____.

4. A _____ is a large mass of sediment deposited
   at the mouth of a river.

5. The dropping of sediment moved by water, wind, and ice is
   called _____.

Use with pages 236–243

How Does Water Shape the Land?

Glossary

clay	a stiff, sticky Earth material that is soft and pilable when wet
floodplain	the land where a river tends to flood
meander	a curve in a river
sand	loose grains or particles of disintegrated rock, finer than rice grains and coarser than silt grains
silt	a material consisting of mineral particles smaller than those of sand and coarser than those of clay

Use the words from the box to complete the paragraphs about rivers.

Deposition helps create a variety of land surface features.

As a river flows over flat land, the river tends to wind in curves

called _____. The river water erodes the outside of

each curve and deposits sediment on the inside.

Sometimes water overflows the river's banks, or floods.

The land where a river tends to flood is called a _____.

Rivers deposit _____, _____, and _____

in floodplains.

**Vocabulary Skill:
Words in Context**

**Tell how you could figure out the meaning of the word *recreational*
in this sentence.**

A river provides recreational opportunities such as boating, fishing, and swimming.

_____

_____

_____

Study Guide
89
Use with pages 236–243

How Do Ice and Wind Shape the Land?

Main Idea Glaciers, which are moving rivers of ice, and wind slowly wear down and build up the land.

- As glaciers move across the land, they carry away tons of soil and rock.

- When glaciers stop moving and begin to melt, they deposit boulders, rocks, and soil.

- Wind picks up sediment from one place and deposits it in another place.

A. Complete the diagram to tell about glaciers.

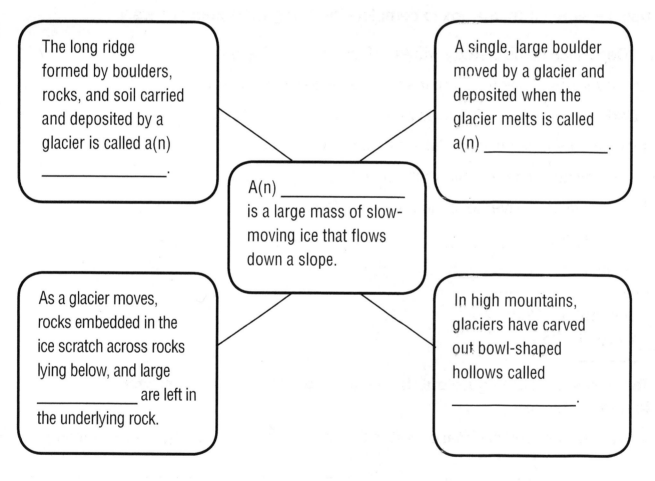

The long ridge formed by boulders, rocks, and soil carried and deposited by a glacier is called a(n) _____.

A single, large boulder moved by a glacier and deposited when the glacier melts is called a(n) _____.

A(n) _____ is a large mass of slow-moving ice that flows down a slope.

As a glacier moves, rocks embedded in the ice scratch across rocks lying below, and large _____ are left in the underlying rock.

In high mountains, glaciers have carved out bowl-shaped hollows called _____.

How Do Ice and Wind Shape the Land?

B. Explain how glaciers carry away and deposit material.

_____

_____

_____

C. Rewrite each statement about how wind shapes the land to make it true.

1. Although it is much stronger than water, wind can change the shape of the land.

_____

_____

2. The stronger the wind, the less sand from beaches and deserts the wind can carry away.

_____

_____

3. Wind erosion is even more likely to cause erosion during a rainy period.

_____

_____

4. Windbreaks, such as buttes and sandstone towers, can prevent or reduce wind erosion.

_____

_____

5. Sediments that the wind carries have little effect on Earth's surface.

_____

_____

How Do Ice and Wind Shape the Land?

erratic   moraine   sand dune

Use the words in the box to complete each sentence.

A(n) _____ is a hill or pile of
sand that was formed by wind.

A single, large boulder moved by a
glacier and deposited when the glacier
melts is called a(n) _____.

The long ridge formed by boulders, rocks,
and soil carried and deposited by a
glacier is called a(n) _____.

How Do Ice and Wind Shape the Land?

Glossary

boulder	a large, rounded mass of rock lying on the ground or imbedded in the soil
groove	a long, narrow furrow or channel
hollow	an opening or space; a small valley
ridge	a long, narrow top or crest of a mountain

Use the words from the box to complete each sentence to tell how ice and wind shape the land. Then circle the words in the puzzle.

a	m	j	o	g	a	w	s	o	g
t	l	u	w	r	v	o	l	m	p
s	e	f	b	o	u	l	d	e	r
u	n	s	p	o	w	l	a	n	s
i	g	e	l	v	x	o	q	z	i
k	h	q	r	e	m	h	r	p	a
l	s	e	g	d	i	r	o	m	e

1. The long _____ formed by boulders, rocks, and soil carried and deposited by a glacier is called a moraine.

2. A single, large _____ moved by a glacier and deposited when the glacier melts is called an erratic.

3. A bowl-shaped _____ left by a glacier is called a cirque.

4. Large _____ left in the underlying rock can show the direction of glacier movement.

Homework: Use the library or Internet to research how glaciers have changed the land in California. Write a paragraph that summarizes what you have learned.

How Do Charges Behave?

Main Idea All objects are made up of tiny particles. Some of these tiny particles carry positive or negative electric charges. An object can be neutral or have a total negative or positive charge.

- Atoms are made up of tiny particles, many of which carry electric charges.

- Objects with like charges repel each other. Objects with unlike charges attract each other.

- Static electricity can discharge when a negatively charged object comes near another object.

A. Complete the diagram to tell about atoms.

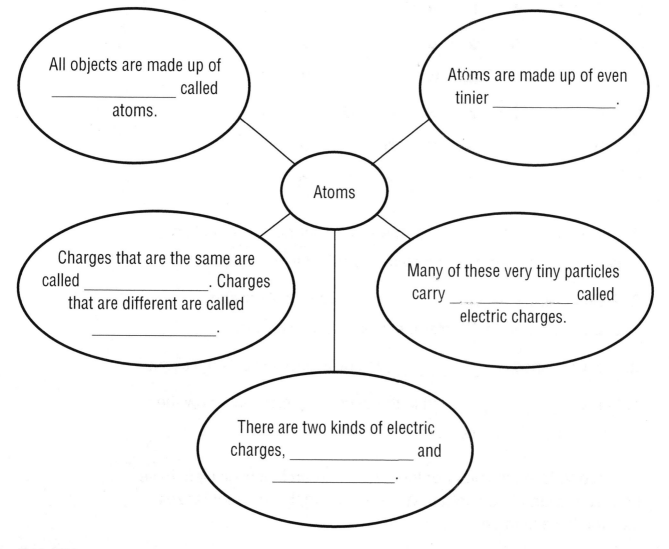

All objects are made up of _____ called atoms.

Atoms are made up of even tinier _____.

Atoms

Charges that are the same are called _____. Charges that are different are called _____.

Many of these very tiny particles carry _____ called electric charges.

There are two kinds of electric charges, _____ and _____.

How Do Charges Behave?

B. Complete the outline to tell about electric charges.

Electric Charges

    I. There are like and unlike _____ charges.

        A. Objects with like charges will _____
        _____.

        B. Objects with unlike charges will _____
        _____.

    II. Negative charged particles respond _____ from
        positive charged particles.

        A. Negative charges will move _____ from one
        material to another.

        B. Negative charges are able to move to a material or object that
        has _____.

**C. Number the events about electric discharge to show the
order in which they happen.**

_____ The boy's body becomes negatively charged.

_____ He gets a shock as a discharge of static electricity occurs.

_____ The boy reaches for a metal doorknob.

_____ A negative charges builds up on his shoes.

_____ A boy walks across a carpet.

How Do Charges Behave?

| electric charges   static electricity |

A. Use a word from the box to complete each sentence.

1. A charge that builds up on a material is called

_____ .

2. Units of electricity carried by very tiny particles are

_____ .

B. Decide whether each word or phrase below is an example of electric charges or static electricity. Then write each word or phrase in the correct box.

hair stands on end and moves towards a comb

negative charges

positive charges

person gets a shock when touching a doorknob

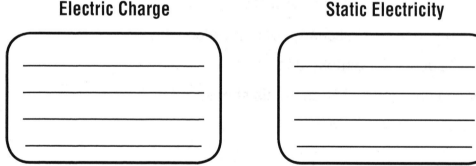

Electric Charge   **Static Electricity**

How Do Charges Behave?

Glossary

discharge	a release of an electric charge
electric	has energy carried by electrons, protons and other particles
material	a substance or object
units	fixed quantities used to measure something

Complete the diagram to tell about electric charges.

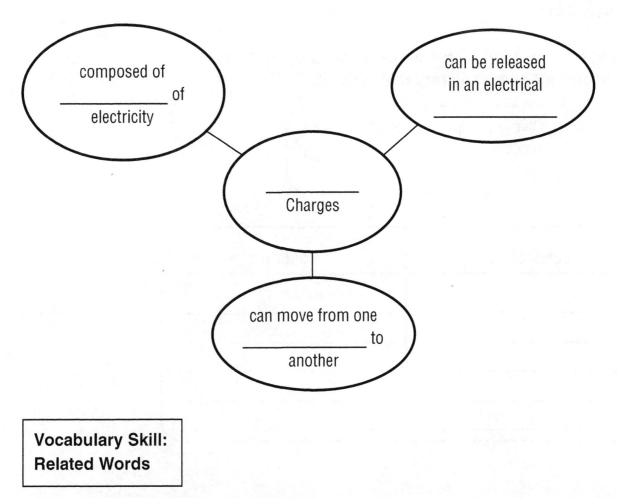

**Vocabulary Skill:
Related Words**

Particle and *particular* are related words. Use a dictionary to find the word root they share and the meaning of this root.

_____

_____

What Is Electric Current?

Main Idea An electric current is a pathway that electric charges follow. Electric circuits can be used to change electrical energy into other forms of energy.

- Electric current can be converted to heat, light, and other forms of energy.

- A loop that an electric current can follow is called an electric circuit. Electric circuits can be series circuits or parallel circuits.

- Electric current can be dangerous. Always follow electric safety rules.

A. Complete the chart with the words that are conductors of electric current and insulators that resist it.

tap water	living things	plastic	gold
rubber	copper	air	
silver	pure water	wood	

Conductors	Insulators
_____	_____
_____	_____
_____	_____
_____	_____

What Is Electric Current?

B. Complete the diagram to tell about electric circuits.

The _____ that electric current follows is an electric circuit.

If there is a _____ in the circuit, you have an open or incomplete circuit.

Most circuits include a switch that _____.

In a series circuit, the electric current passes along _____.

In a parallel circuit, the electric current passes along _____.

C. Rewrite each statement about electric safety to make it true.

1. Never touch insulated electric wires.

_____

_____

2. When too little electric current flows through an object, the object can heat up.

_____

_____

3. Never put anything except a metal object inside an outlet.

_____

_____

What Is Electric Current?

> battery   electric circuit   insulator   series circuit
> conductor electric current   parallel circuit

Complete the diagram using the words from the box.

A _____ is where the current passes through each part along a single pathway.

Each _____ has a power source, such as a _____ and a _____ such as wire, which may be covered by rubber that acts as an _____.

Each circuit has an object that uses _____.

A _____ is where current passes along more than one pathway.

Homework: Design a flyer to promote electrical safety in your school. Use both words and images to tell about ways that fellow students can stay safe.

What is Electric Current?

Glossary

closed circuit	an electric circuit through which current can flow in an uninterrupted path
flashlight	a battery-operated portable light
light bulb	a glass bulb providing light when electric current is passed through
pathway	a path or course

Use the words from the box to complete the paragraph about electric circuits.

One or more batteries form part of the circuit in a _____.
A metal spring and a metal case around the batteries carry current
to the _____. The electric circuit is the _____
the current flows through. When you press the ON button, you create
a _____, causing the light to shine.

**Vocabulary Skill:
Compound Words**

The words in the box are compound words. Explain how you can determine the meaning of each compound word in the following sentences.

1. Electric current follows a pathway from one place to another.

   _____

   _____

2. The flashlight has run out of batteries.

   _____

   _____

   _____

How Is Electricity Used?

Main Idea When people use electric current, they change the electrical energy to heat, light energy, and the energy of motion.

- Electrical energy can be converted into heat.
- Electrical energy can be converted into light.
- Electrical energy can be converted into the energy of motion.

A. Complete the chart with the words from the box to tell about different kinds of electrical use.

toasters	cars	light	wheelchairs
radios	hair dryers	microwave ovens	stereos

Kinds of Electrical Energy	Examples
Sound	_____
Heat	_____
_____	computer monitor, television, lasers
Motion	_____

How Is Electricity Used?

B. Number the events about using a light bulb in the order in which they occur.

_____ As the material heats up, it begins to glow brightly.

_____ Electric current flows into the device through an electric cord.

_____ Light is created.

_____ The resistance causes the material to heat up.

_____ The current passes through a material that has resistance.

C. Put a check next to each statement about electric energy usage that is true.

_____ Power companies use watts to measure how much electrical energy is used in a home.

_____ Running an electric clothes dryer for an hour uses the same amount of energy as turning on a light bulb for an hour.

_____ When an electric current meets resistance, the material begins to heat up.

_____ A light bulb creates light in a completely different way than a heating unit creates heat.

_____ Different electrical devices use the same amounts of electricity.

_____ Heating units in electrical devices can get very hot.

_____ Power tools convert electricity to motion.

Use with pages 290–297

How Is Electricity Used?

resistance   watt

Use the words in the box to complete each sentence.

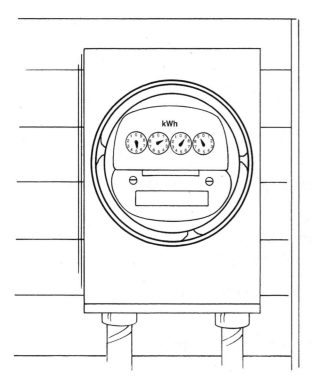

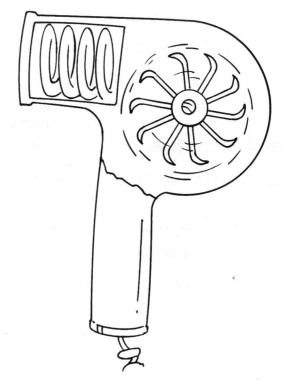

Electric meters measure how much electric energy is being used in a house using a unit called a _____.

This hair dryer's coils have a _____ or ability to slow down electric current, causing the coils to heat up.

Homework: Imagine that there was no resistance in electric devices used for heating. Write a paragraph describing what would happen and explain why it would happen.

How Is Energy Used?

Glossary

devices	machines with a particular purpose
fluorescent light	a kind of electric light that uses gas
gas	a form of matter that has no definite shape or volume
scooters	one-person vehicles with a narrow foot board and two wheels
vehicles	devices used for transportation

Use a word from the box to rewrite each sentence about electric energy to make it true.

1. Electrical powers can convert electricity into motion and light.

_____

_____

2. A number of appliances use electric energy to turn wheels and create motion.

_____

_____

3. One example of this is hang gliders.

_____

_____

4. A radio converts electric energy to light.

_____

_____

5. It works by passing an electric current through a special solid.

_____

_____

How Do Magnets Behave?

Main Idea Magnets are objects that attract certain materials such as iron. Magnets have magnetic poles and magnetic fields where the magnetic force acts.

- A magnet is an object that attracts objects made of iron, steel, and other metals.

- Magnets have a north pole and a south pole. Unlike poles attract each other, and like poles repel each other.

- The force of a magnet can act within the magnetic field.

A. Complete the chart with the words from the box to tell about the objects that magnets can attract. Then answer the question that follows.

> plastic   iron
> wood   steel
> rubber   other metals

Magnets Attract

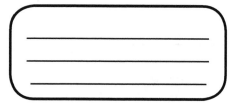

Magnets Do Not Attract

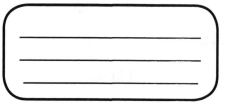

What happens to the force of magnetism on objects as the distance from the magnet increases?

_____

_____

How Do Magnets Behave?

B. Rewrite each statement about magnets to make it true.

1. Magnets stick to most refrigerators because the doors are made of steel, which contains silver.

   _____

   _____

2. Temporary magnets keep their magnetism for a long time.

   _____

   _____

3. You can magnetize some objects to make them permanent magnets.

   _____

   _____

C. Complete the diagram to tell about magnetism.

These are _____.
The magnetic poles are

_____.

The poles are where the force of this magnet is the

_____.

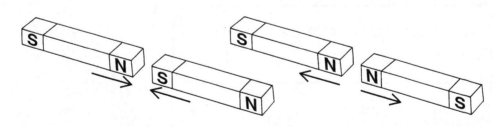

These unlike poles _____.

The like poles in this magnet _____.

How Do Magnets Behave?

> magnet   magnetic poles   temporary magnet
> magnetic field   permanent magnet

Use the words in the box to complete the diagram that tells about creating a magnet.

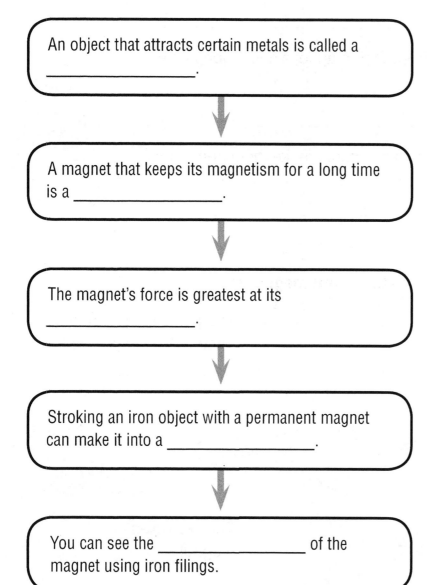

An object that attracts certain metals is called a _____.

A magnet that keeps its magnetism for a long time is a _____.

The magnet's force is greatest at its _____.

Stroking an iron object with a permanent magnet can make it into a _____.

You can see the _____ of the magnet using iron filings.

Study Guide
108
Use with pages 308–313

How Do Magnets Behave?

Glossary

attracted	caused to draw near or adhere
filings	tiny particles
force	strength; power; energy

Use the words from the box to complete the chart.

Observation	Explanation
If you hold a magnet far away from the steel on a refrigerator, the magnet and the steel will not be strongly _____.	The _____ of magnetism on objects decreases as the distance from the magnet increases.
When you pour iron _____ over a bar magnet, the filings are thicker and closer together at the poles of a magnet.	The magnetic _____ is stronger closer to the magnet and near the poles than it is farther away.

Vocabulary Skill:
Word Parts

Filings is related to the word *file*. A file is a steel tool used to wear away hard substances. Based on this information, write your own definition of *filings*.

_____

_____

Study Guide
109
Use with pages 308–313

Name _____ Date _____

What Is Earth's Magnetic Field?

Main Idea Earth acts like a giant magnet, with a magnetic field and magnetic poles. This allows compasses to work and causes many effects on and around Earth.

- Earth acts like a giant magnet because of Earth's iron core, which is magnetized.

- The north-seeking poles of a compass needle and other magnets on Earth are attracted to Earth's north magnetic pole.

- Auroras, caused by Earth's magnetic field, are created when particles from the Sun collide with particles in Earth's atmosphere.

A. Complete the diagram by filling in the blanks.

Earth's center is made up mostly of   This action produces Earth's

_____ .   _____ .

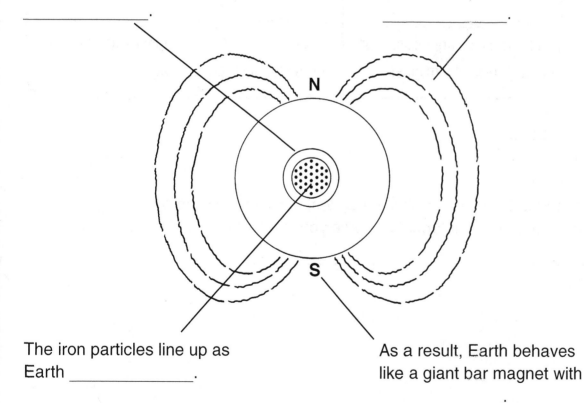

The iron particles line up as   As a result, Earth behaves
Earth _____ .   like a giant bar magnet with

                                           _____ .

What Is Earth's Magnetic Field?

B. Rewrite each statement about magnets to make it true.

1. A compass senses magnetic south using a free-moving magnet.

   _____

   _____

2. The needle of a magnetic compass is a temporary magnet.

   _____

   _____

3. The north-seeking pole of the needle will turn until it points away from the magnetic north pole of Earth.

   _____

   _____

4. The magnetic north pole is exactly over Earth's geographic North Pole.

   _____

   _____

C. Number the events in order to tell about how auroras form.

_____ The particles collide with the top of Earth's atmosphere.

_____ The particles are pulled toward the magnetic force at Earth's magnetic poles.

_____ The Sun sends out waves of tiny particles.

_____ The colliding particles begin to glow.

_____ Earth's magnetic field captures some of the particles.

What Is Earth's Magnetic Field?

compass   aurora

A. Put a check next to each true statement about a compass.

_____ A compass is an instrument that senses magnetic north using a free-moving magnet.

_____ The south-seeking pole of a compass needle will point toward the magnetic north pole of Earth.

_____ Thousands of years ago, Chinese sailors used lodestone to create compasses.

_____ Today's sailors no longer use compasses.

_____ The needle of a magnetic compass is a permanent magnet.

B. Put a check next to each true statement about auroras.

_____ Auroras are a display of lights in the sky.

_____ Auroras occur along Earth's equator.

_____ Auroras are caused by particles from the Sun interacting with Earth's magnetic field and atmosphere.

_____ Auroras are often called "northern lights" or "southern lights."

_____ Auroras occur because particles from the Sun are attracted by Earth's atmosphere.

Homework: Use the library or the Internet to find out more about the early compasses that sailors used to navigate their ships. Write a paragraph summarizing what you learned.

Name _____ Date _____

What Is Earth's Magnetic Field?

Glossary

core	central region of the Earth
geographic	of or relating to geography
molten	made into liquid by heat

Use the words in the box to complete the diagram.

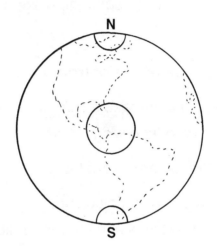

Cause   **Effect**

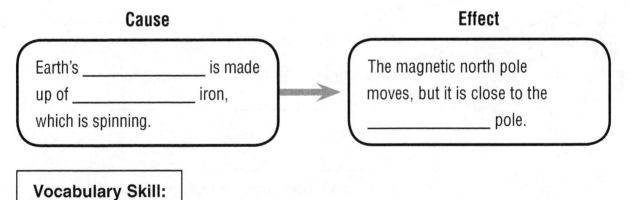

Earth's _____ is made up of _____ iron, which is spinning.

The magnetic north pole moves, but it is close to the _____ pole.

┌─────────────────────┐
│ **Vocabulary Skill:** │
│ **Word Parts** │
└─────────────────────┘

The prefix *geo-* means "earth" and the word root *graph* is related to studying or writing. Using this information, write your own definition of *geography*.

_____

_____

How Are Electromagnets Used?

Main Idea Electricity can produce magnetism, and magnetism can produce electricity.

- An electromagnet is a temporary magnet formed when an electric current travels around a magnetic material such as iron.

- Motors use electromagnets and permanent magnets to change electricity into the energy of motion.

- Generators turn motion into electricity by spinning magnets around wires.

A. Complete the diagram to describe how electromagnets are made.

You can make a magnet by using _____ to produce magnetism.

An electromagnet is a _____.

When electric current _____ it produces a weak magnetic field.

If the wire is _____, the iron becomes magnetized.

Increasing the number of wire coils will

_____.

Increasing

_____

will also increase the strength of the electromagnet.

When the electric current is turned off, the electromagnet _____.

How Are Electromagnets Used?

B. Complete the diagram to tell how an electric motor works.

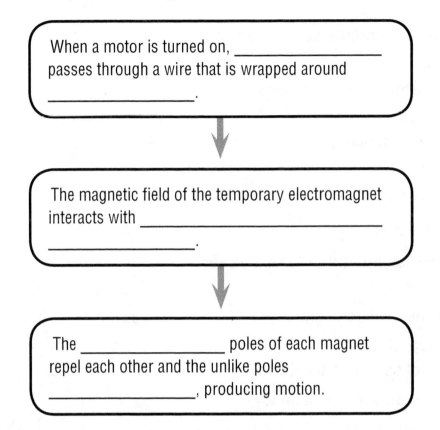

When a motor is turned on, _____ passes through a wire that is wrapped around _____.

The magnetic field of the temporary electromagnet interacts with _____ _____.

The _____ poles of each magnet repel each other and the unlike poles _____, producing motion.

C. Complete the diagram about generators.

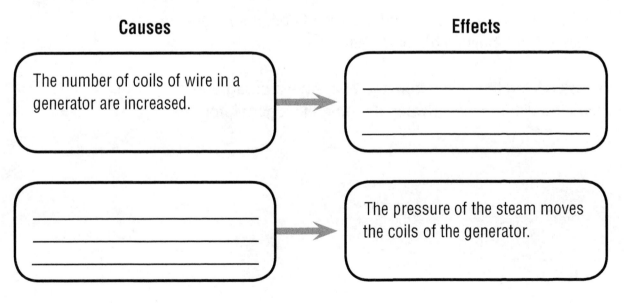

Causes

The number of coils of wire in a generator are increased.

Effects

_____
_____
_____

_____
_____
_____

The pressure of the steam moves the coils of the generator.

Use with pages 322–329

How Are Electromagnets Used?

> electromagnet   generator   motor

A. Use a word from the box to complete each sentence about electromagnetism.

1. A device that uses magnetism to convert energy of motion into electrical energy is a(n) _____.

2. A device that changes electrical energy into energy of motion is an electric _____.

3. A strong temporary magnet that uses electricity to produce magnetism is a(n) _____.

B. Put a check next to each statement that is true about electromagnetism.

_____ All electric motors contain electromagnets and permanent magnets.

_____ An electromagnet cannot be turned on and off.

_____ A generator and a motor work in the same way.

_____ When electric current passes through a wire, the current produces a weak magnetic field around the wire.

_____ If the wire is wrapped around a piece of iron, the magnetic field around the wire becomes stronger.

Homework: Using the words from the box, write a paragraph explaining the differences between a motor and a generator.

How Are Electromagnets Used?

Glossary

appliances	devices or machines for household use
efficiently	acting or producing effectively with a minimum of waste
refrigerator	a box-like appliance used to keep food fresh
wastes	uses without adequate return

Use the words in the box to complete the diagram to tell about the cost of using electricity.

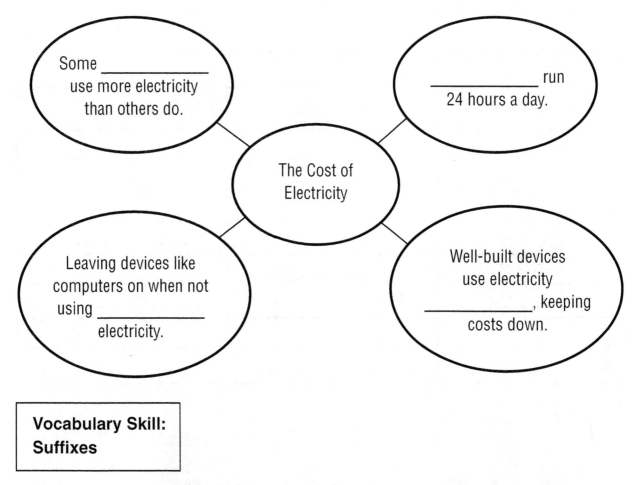

Some _____ use more electricity than others do.

_____ run 24 hours a day.

The Cost of Electricity

Leaving devices like computers on when not using _____ electricity.

Well-built devices use electricity _____, keeping costs down.

Vocabulary Skill: Suffixes

When the suffix -*ly* is added to an adjective, it forms an adverb. The suffix usually indicates the manner or way in which an action is performed. If *efficient* means "productive with a minimum of waste," what does *efficiently* mean?

_____

_____

How Can Energy Be Conserved?

Main Idea Electricity uses natural resources. Conserving electricity helps save natural resources. Finding alternate sources of electrical energy can also prevent pollution.

- Most electricity in the United States is generated using fossil fuels.

- Other sources of energy include hydroelectric power, wind power, and solar power.

- You can conserve electricity by turning off devices when they are not in use and following other tips.

A. Complete the chart to tell about alternate energy sources.

Energy Source	Description	Example
Hydroelectric power	_____ _____	_____ _____
Wind power	_____ _____	_____ _____
_____ _____	uses energy from heat within Earth	_____ _____
Solar power	_____ _____	_____ _____

How Can Energy Be Conserved?

B. Complete the flow chart about wind power.

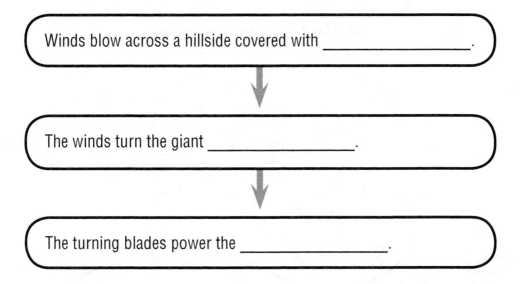

Winds blow across a hillside covered with _____.

The winds turn the giant _____.

The turning blades power the _____.

C. Rewrite each statement about conserving electricity to make it true.

1. One of the best ways to reduce pollution and use resources is to conserve electricity.

   _____

   _____

2. Don't leave the washing machine door open any longer than you have to.

   _____

   _____

3. Use hot water whenever possible.

   _____

   _____

4. Turn on TVs, radios, and stereos when no one is using them.

   _____

   _____

How Can Energy Be Conserved?

fossil fuels

Complete the diagram about fossil fuels by filling in the blanks.

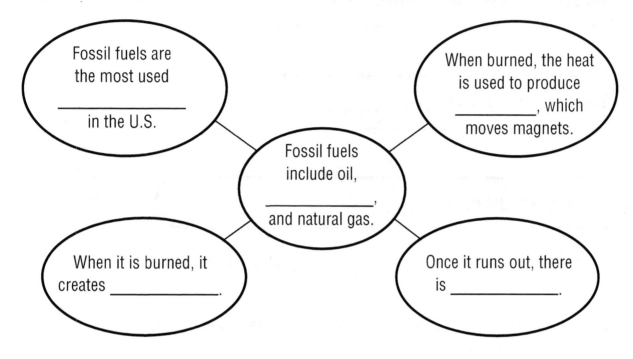

Fossil fuels are the most used _____ in the U.S.

When burned, the heat is used to produce _____, which moves magnets.

Fossil fuels include oil, _____, and natural gas.

When it is burned, it creates _____.

Once it runs out, there is _____.

Homework: Write a letter to the editor of your local newspaper explaining how you feel about fossil fuels and alternate energy sources.

How Can Energy Be Conserved?

Glossary

coal	dark substance burned as fuel
poisonous	deadly; hazardous to health
soot	black powder produced by burning coal
steam	water in the form of gas

Complete the outline with a word from the box to tell about fossil fuels.

I. The Need for Fossil Fuels

   A. It takes energy to move the magnets in generators.

   B. Fossil fuels, natural fuels such as _____ or oil, are burned to heat water to create _____ .

II. Disadvantages of Using Fossil Fuels

   A. The supply of fossil fuels is limited.

   B. Burning fossil fuels creates pollution.

      1. _____ , smoke, and _____ gases

Vocabulary Skill: Sentence Context

You can often figure out the meaning of new words by looking for clues in the text. What clues help you figure out the meaning of *poisonous*?

Burning fossil fuels also creates pollution. It adds soot, smoke, and poisonous gases to the air.

_____

_____

_____

_____

4500805216-0607-2020

Printed in the U.S.A